LEADING FROM THE INSIDE OUT

D1445791

TEACHER'S TOOLKIT SERIES

LEADING FROM THE INSIDE OUT

Expanded Roles for Teachers

in Equitable Schools

W. Norton Grubb and Lynda Tredway

TEACHER'S TOOLKIT SERIES

Paradigm Publishers
Boulder • London

Copyright © 2010 Paradigm Publishers

Published in the United States by Paradigm Publishers, 2845 Wilderness Place, Suite 200, Boulder, CO 80301 USA.

Paradigm Publishers is the trade name of Birkenkamp & Company, LLC, Dean Birkenkamp, President and Publisher.

Library of Congress Cataloging-in-Publication Data

Grubb, W. Norton.
 Leading from the inside out : expanded roles for teachers in equitable schools / W. Norton Grubb and Lynda Tredway.
 p. cm.
 Includes bibliographical references and index.
 ISBN 978-1-59451-836-2 (pbk. : alk. paper)
 1. Teacher participation in administration—United States. 2. Educational equal-ization—United States. 3. School improvement programs—United States. I. Tred-way, Lynda. II. Title.
 LB2806.45.G78 2010
 371.1'06—dc22
                                2010002463

Printed and bound in the United States of America on acid-free paper that meets the standards of the American National Standard for Permanence of Paper for Printed Library Materials.

Design by Cindy Young.

14 13 12 11 10   1 2 3 4 5

CONTENTS

SERIES FOREWORD

THIS TEACHER'S TOOLKIT series is a set of six related books written for prospective, new, and experienced teachers who are committed to students and families, who conceive of themselves as agents of democratic change, and who are eager to think more deeply, more broadly, and more practically about their work in education. All six books succinctly link theory with practice, present extended arguments for improving education, and wrap their discussions around successful examples of the topics in question.

Although each book is its own resource, the books in the Toolkit series share some common views about teaching. For one, all of the books treat teachers not as mere deliverers of curriculum but as active, three-dimensional professionals capable of diagnosing student learning, developing powerful educational experiences, assessing and adjusting student learning, and forming productive relationships with children and adults in schools. Another view all of the books share is that teaching is hard work that is among the most important kinds of work any society requires. My grandmother used to say that no society can survive without farmers or teachers. I think that is still true. Teaching is undeniably difficult work, but it is also frequently enjoyable work because it is so challenging, meaningful, and success oriented. These books are for teachers who have accepted the challenges of teaching because they relish the satisfaction of the work, they enjoy helping young people grow, and they know that quality education is necessary for the health of our world.

A third commonality about teaching among these books is their shared presumption that teachers are always looking for ways to improve. Teaching is a profession in which one enters as a novice, develops expertise over time, and continues to grow and change throughout the whole of one's career. The Toolkit books are written for teachers at multiple points in their career cycle: Beginning teachers will learn new ways to think about learning, students, and what it means to become a successful educator. Early- and middle-career teachers can reflect on their own practice in light of the ideas, strategies, and stories of these books—and they can use the books to deepen and broaden their future work. Veteran teachers can see themselves and their varied experiences inside the perspectives of the books, as well as figure out how they can continue to challenge themselves and their students—and perhaps take on other kinds of education work such as mentoring newer teachers, advocating for students on a broader stage, or writing about their own teaching. No matter where readers are in their education careers, these books offer powerful learning and useful opportunities for professional reflection.

The six books are sequenced to loosely follow both the career cycle of teaching and the fact that, as teachers progress, they often widen their sphere of influence. Book 1 in the series is *Teaching for Success: Developing Your Teacher Identity in Today's Classroom* by Brad Olsen. This book focuses on the processes of "becoming a teacher" and explores how to teach well in this contemporary age. Wrapping its conversations about teacher development around the core concept of teacher identity, the book offers its own teacher learning experience: how to recognize, adjust, and maximize the many ways your personal self and your professional self become integrated in your teaching work.

Book 2, *Teaching English Learners: Fostering Language and the Democratic Experience*, by Kip Téllez, focuses on what teachers can do in their classrooms in order to better understand and more effectively teach English learners. Drawing from research and experience not only on learning and teaching but also on culture, language, immigration, and contemporary politics, Téllez offers a unique guide for use by U.S. teachers interested in deeply and compassionately supporting the growth of students whose native language is not English.

Book 3 in the series is *Teaching Without Bells: What We Can Learn from Powerful Instruction in Small Schools* by Joey Feldman. This book offers a valuable look at how teaching and learning are fundamentally influenced by school size. The book's premise is that student and teacher experiences in education are direct functions of their school's size (and its accompanying influence on how schools are organized). Focusing on challenges and benefits of teaching in small high schools, Feldman's book helps readers consider where they might want to teach and—no matter the size of their school site—how they can teach well by maximizing lessons from the small schools movement.

Book 4, *Leading from the Inside Out: Expanded Roles for Teachers in Equitable Schools*, by Norton Grubb and Lynda Tredway, opens up the professional world of the teacher by offering new ways to think about school reform from the vantage point of the teacher. The authors make a compelling case for teachers as the key ingredient in education reform and schools as the lever for democratic educational change. Presenting a blueprint for a new kind of school in which teachers are not only classroom instructors but education reformers as well, Grubb and Tredway illustrate why we have the schools we have today and how broad-minded teachers can transform them into successful schools for tomorrow.

Book 5, *Teaching Toward Democracy: Educators as Agents of Change*, by William Ayers, Kevin Kumashiro, Erica Meiners, Therese Quinn, and David Stovall, also considers teachers as agents of change on a broader scale. The authors share their ideas about how teachers can better humanize schooling for students, combat some of the current failings of market models of education, and extend their teaching work past the school day and outside the school walls. Their book invites readers into a view of education through the eyes of students, and it provides thoughtful strategies to enact teaching for social justice as not just a popular slogan but as an authentic focus on human rights and social equity for all.

And, to close out the series, Book 6, *Making a Difference: Developing Meaningful Careers in Education*, by Karen Hunter Quartz, Brad Olsen, Lauren Anderson, and Kimberly Barraza Lyons, looks at whole careers in education. This book examines the dynamic lives and work of several educators in Los Angeles and investigates why teachers stay in the classroom or shift to other kinds of education roles, such as school administrator, curriculum coordinator, or teacher mentor. The book unpacks the sometimes maddening complexity of the teaching profession and offers a roadmap for how teachers can, themselves, remain challenged and satisfied as educators without relaxing their commitments to students.

There are different approaches to reading the books in this series. One way is to consider the whole series as a coherent set of sequenced conversations about teaching. In this manner, you might read the books one at a time, all the way through, inserting yourself into the text of the books: Do the stories and experiences in the books ring true for you? How will you use these books to improve your practice, broaden your influence, and deepen your professional satisfaction? You might imagine, as you read the books this way, that you are sitting in a room with the authors—listening to their ideas, questioning them, actively engaging with their arguments, or talking back to the text when necessary.

Or perhaps you might use these books as textbooks—as thoughtful primers on selected topics that interest you. In this manner, you might pick and choose particular chapters to study: Which specific ideas will you implement in your teaching tomorrow? Are there further readings or key resources that you will hunt down and look at on your own? What concrete activities will you try out? Write notes in the margins of the books and return to the chapters regularly. Photocopy single pages (not whole chapters, please!) to share with peers. Use the books as you plan lessons or design curricula. Engage with the reflection questions at the end of each book's chapters. You will find occasionally in the margins cross-references on specific topics to other books in the series. When you read "Cross-Reference, See Book 2 ..." you can use the numbered list of titles on p. ii to correlate each reference to the intended book.

Or, you may pick some of the books to read collectively with other educators—maybe with your teacher education cohort, or as a group of teachers working with a mentor, or perhaps as part of a teacher inquiry group that you set up with colleagues. Group discussion of these books allows their arguments, perspectives, and examples to prompt your own collective reflection and professional growth: What themes from the books call out to you? What points might you disagree with? How might different educators among you interpret parts of these books in different, perhaps competing, ways? How can these books inspire you to create specific collaborative projects or teacher networks at your school site? You may find the reflection questions at the end of each chapter particularly useful for group conversation.

This series of books is called the "Teacher's Toolkit," but maybe, for some, the idea of a *toolkit* for teachers may not, at first glance, be apt. Picturing a toolkit could conjure images of a steel toolbox or super-hero's belt full of hardware for educators—a diagnostic screwdriver, the clawhammer of homework, a set of precision wrenches for adjusting student learning on the fly. Such images are, well, just too instrumental. They risk suggesting that teaching is mechanical or automatic, or that what good educators do is select utensils from their box to apply when needed. That doesn't describe the kind of teaching I know and love. It erroneously suggests that students are to be fastened with bolts or hammered into obedience, or that learning is gut-wrenchingly rigid. And, to my mind, such a view treats teachers as technicians trained by rote, using tools given to them by others, following directions written on the outside of the box.

Instead, the authors of these books conceive of education as less fixed, more fluid, less finished, more uncertain, and certainly far more complicated than anything for which traditional tools would work. These authors—based on their own years of experience as classroom teachers, educational researchers, school administrators, and university professors—view education similarly to educational philosopher John Dewey when, in 1934, he wrote:

> About 40 years ago, a new idea dawned in education. Educators began to see that education should parallel life, that the school should reproduce the child's world. In this new type of education the child, instead of the curriculum, became the centre of interest, and since the child is active, changing, creative—education ceased to be static, [and] became dynamic and creative in response to the needs of the child.[1]

Like Dewey, I understand teaching and learning to be context-specific, highly creative, dynamically student-centered activities that are as complicated and multifaceted as life itself. And just as important.

So let's reimagine the analogy of a teacher's toolkit. A *toolkit* for teachers could instead be a metaphor for a thoughtful, useful, provocative bundle of perspectives, theories, and approaches for teachers—a set of lively teaching discussions written by different authors who share some common ground. This bundle would empathize with teachers since its authors are all teachers, as well as education researchers and writers: they know both how difficult and how rewarding teaching can be. But it would also exhort teachers not to fall down on the job—not to shirk their work, make excuses, or lessen their resolve to support students.

The bundle of teaching conversations could share stories from the classroom that reveal teaching to be kaleidoscopic: made up of thousands of shifting views, hundreds of competing relations, and dozens of different ways to succeed with children. The stories would reveal how to be a great teacher and why doing so is so damned important. The bundle of ideas and perspectives would include actual examples of good teaching, lesson ideas, and lots of research tidbits useful for prospective and practicing educators. Yes, that could be a toolkit I would want to own. It would be a kit full of thoughtful perspectives, research summaries, wisdom of practice, and impassioned words of advice from handpicked educationalists. An "idea kit," really. A boxed set of thoughtful primers on how to teach well for social change in the current global climate.

John Dewey famously built up binaries in his writing—teaching is either this or that; students learn in this way but not in that way—only to collapse the binary in the end and suggest that education is too complicated for easy contradictions. So I'll take a page from Dewey's playbook and attempt the same. Maybe we can consider this book series as not an either/or. Not as *either* a box of teaching instruments *or* a collection of thoughtful conversations about education, but as both: a set of tangible strategies for teachers to make their own and a loosely bundled collection of professional arguments for use by educators in order to think for themselves, but in deeper and newer ways than before. That's the way that I prefer to envision this teacher's toolkit.

No matter how you choose to make use of the books in the Teacher's Toolkit, it is our sincere hope that you will find value in them. We have tried to make them accessible, conversational, substantive, and succinct. We all believe that teaching is a fundamentally important profession, and, if this world is to improve and grow, it will be because our teachers can help future generations to become wise, creative, and critical thinkers who put their ideas into action toward improving the societies they will inherit. You are an essential part of that human process.

—Brad Olsen
University of California, Santa Cruz

NOTE

1. Dewey, J. 1934. "Tomorrow May Be Too Late: Save the Schools Now." Reprinted in J. Boydston (ed.), *John Dewey: The Later Works, 1925–1953: 1933–1934, Vol. 9* (Carbondale: Southern Illinois University Press, 1986), 386.

CHAPTER ONE

INTRODUCTION

The Personal and the Institutional

O N ANY GIVEN DAY, over one-quarter of the children and adults in the United States are going to school or working in a school or district. The ways schools and the people in them interact are enormously important to their daily lives, as well as to the futures of children and of the country. The lion's share of these adults are teachers in classrooms, and the contention of this book is that any lasting change must come from the inside out—from teachers acting together inside their schools and then moving outside the school to other arenas of advocacy and political participation. Even within their schools, teachers can play new roles, working with one another and with leaders to develop equitable schools: schools that prepare *all* their students for the civic, community, family, occupational, and intellectual roles they will play as adults in the twenty-first century of increasing complexity. We sometimes call these *collective* or *collaborative schools*, because we are convinced by the evidence throughout this book that equitable schools cannot be created without the collective

1

actions of teachers as classroom and school leaders, working together and working with other leaders to solve their own problems. Of course, teachers and leaders operate within the larger context of policy and other social influences, and educators need to know how these external influences on schools work if they are to act outside as well as inside schools to support change. This book therefore provides the building blocks of history, policy, and social analysis that are necessary for turning teachers into the teacher-leaders needed for equitable and collective schools—places where adults thrive as learners and are able in turn to create joyful learning experiences for children and youth.

Educators often think of schooling as a question of personal relationships, in which the connection between teacher and student is at the heart of learning; a common phrase is "it's all about relationships." A current phrase for a strong teacher is "warm demander," meaning that the teacher builds supportive relationships with students at the same time he or she maintains high expectations for student learning. Within this perspective, principals and other administrators stress the personal characteristics of the teachers they hire, their energy and charisma, insisting that "good teachers are born, not made." The search in school reform for "good teaching" focuses on identifying the individual characteristics of effective teachers—whether they have certain credentials or not, or whether years of experience matter. We give out awards to individual good teachers—to district- or state-level Teachers of the Year—as if "good teaching" were the result of individual dedication and ability, rather than rewarding *schools* that have nurtured larger numbers of effective teachers. And, for those readers who are new teachers, virtually all teacher preparation focuses on the capacities of individuals—on mastery of particular teaching techniques, on ways of relating to students, sometimes on classroom management as the responsibility of

**Cross-Reference
See Book 3,
Chapter 2 on
the theory and
practice of
fostering
relationships
with students.**

the individual teacher rather than the responsibility of a school for creating a certain climate.

None of this is wrong, of course: we need skilled teachers who have mastered a range of teaching practices and who have the personal characteristics to empathize with and support students personally as well as intellectually. But it's incomplete, because teachers work their magic within institutions with certain characteristics. The very fact that we have people called "teachers" who are credentialed based on their learning in teacher preparation programs—rather than hired "off the street," as instructors in adult education and job training still are, or chosen for their moral character as teachers once were—is an institutional development that has taken place over more than a century. The limited responsibilities that teachers in most schools have for what happens in the classroom—but not for budget and curriculum decisions—are again an institutional condition that developed over time. The description of teachers as "warm demanders" suggests standards that determine the expectations and demands of teachers, and these usually come from outside the classroom—from a math department articulating its common requirements, or state standards embedded in accountability exams, or the standards articulated by disciplinary groups like the National Council of Teachers of Mathematics (NCTM) or English (NCTE).

Focus point

Schools include other individuals called "principals"—short for "principal teacher," the nineteenth-century title—with different roles and responsibilities and their own forms of credentialing. Many policies affecting the classroom—about curricula, class size, the nature of teacher preparation, the length of the typical class, when school starts in the morning and stops in the afternoon, the school year—are either historical decisions or ones that have evolved over time (for example, the school year is based on nineteenth-century agricultural rhythms). Districts and states have imposed their own layers of decisions, covering levels of funding, the distribution of funding among rich and poor districts, curriculum, and high school graduation requirements. Anyone who has taught in a school receiving federal funds knows about burdensome federal mandates: meeting targets for Annual Yearly Progress (AYP) under No Child Left Behind (NCLB) and following the rigid procedures required for special education students are but two examples. These institutional constraints and practices are part of what David Tyack and Larry Cuban (1995) call the "grammar of schooling," the basic rules and norms by which schools operate—all so familiar that we often fail to think about their particulars.

So schools are about people and relationships, but they are not *all* about people; they are also about institutions. At least in modern societies, the informal or "natural" places for learning—families, where sons learn from fathers and daughters from their mothers, or apprenticeships, where inexperienced workers learn from masters—don't work the ways they did previously, and in some cases (such as in abusive families or exploitive firms) they do not work well at all. In many cases, they are inequitable and inconsistent as well. Therefore, as Robert Bellah and his colleagues (1985) remind us in trying to counter the extreme individualism of American thinking, "we live through institutions": we create institutions within which individuals can exercise their individual capacities. Tool 1-A provides an exercise in which teachers and leaders can confront the role of individuals within institutions, starting from Bellah's ideas.

This book discusses the institutional issues that confront teachers, teacher-leaders, and even principals as they wrestle with how best to support their development as teachers and as leaders. The issues we raise are therefore not the classroom-level problems of how to teach, how to motivate students, or how to develop supportive personal relations, although we touch on those. (Such fundamental issues are the focus of other books within

Schools are about people and relationships, but they are not *all* about people; they are also about institutions.

this series, as well as of teacher preparation and induction programs.) Instead, our focus is on how teachers can move out of the individual classroom and think collectively about the institution: for example, What schools would they like to work in? What responsibilities do they have for creating such schools? What policies are established outside the school, and how can they influence those policies rather than simply being subjected to them? Our image of a teacher is not someone whose influence is limited to the classroom and students; such an image is an old-fashioned, century-old conception. Rather, we envision schools where teachers vigorously engage in their profession in and out of the classroom, take leadership positions on issues within the school as teacher-leaders, and participate in influencing those external policies (including school reforms) that influence schools. Rather than reinforcing one of the great divides in education—between teachers in their classrooms and individuals outside who may influence classrooms without understanding them well—we prefer to envision roles for teachers that bridge this divide.

"We live through institutions": we create institutions within which individuals can exercise their individual capacities.

In this chapter we first articulate three different kinds of schools—traditional, entrepreneurial, and collective—partly to clarify how different schools can be, and partly to outline the different roles teachers and leaders can play. We then examine two of the most fundamental issues surrounding all schools: their purposes, or why we create these special institutions; and the equity of schools, or who will be included in and well served by them. Teachers may have their own ideas about these ultimate goals, and these may shape individual practices, or even influence where, how, and whom they teach. One teacher may emphasize social studies and citizenship, another science for a technological society; still others may stress the special needs of immigrant students or African American males. But the ability to modify individual classrooms in these ways is limited by various institutional pressures, ranging from required curricula to state-imposed testing.

Recognizing who makes these external decisions is an important step to changing them. In this chapter in particular, then, we raise fundamental questions with which all educators must wrestle. These questions involve the deepest values about our society, and every generation—indeed, every school and every teacher—must come up with its own answers.

ALTERNATIVE MODELS OF SCHOOLS

Even though schools are institutions with particular practices and norms, these institutions take many different forms, and they can certainly change over time. Americans have many different images of schools, some outdated, some more recent. One of the first was the Little Red Schoolhouse, rooted in the local community as the center of town life, with its ability to teach all ages of students in a single classroom but with a teacher only slightly more educated than her students. Moving forward in time, a different image arises—of the urban school with a distinct and imposing architecture, by now with separate classrooms for different ages and grades, with desks bolted to the floor in neat rows designed for students to pay rapt attention to the teacher in the front of the class—the architecture of the teacher-centered classroom. Another image is the well-funded suburban school, often one-story, with different buildings for different purposes (the science labs, the gym, vocational workshops), set on a massive expanse of playing fields and parking, more like a shopping mall than a school (Powell, Farrar, and Cohen 1985). We often face the reality of urban schools, the "blackboard jungles"—dilapidated, overcrowded, with temporary buildings to handle the overflow, opaque windows, and fencing, more like prisons than nurturing places for kids. Occasionally there are beautifully designed schools, reflecting and promoting the instructional activities taking place inside, but these are rare. And various people have proposed schools without buildings, where students are placed in "internships" throughout the community, though these are rarer still.

Although there are almost limitless conceptions of what a school might be, in practice three major approaches to schools help us sort through the possibilities: (1) traditional or conventional, (2) entrepreneurial, and (3) collective or collaborative. We outline these not to suggest that these are the only three that educators might envision but to clarify that the three common approaches make very different assumptions about teachers, their preparation, and the level of teacher responsibility for developing practices.

The *traditional* or conventional model of schooling is the one most of us are familiar with. Emerging in the nineteenth century, it was reinforced by educational administrators between 1900 and 1920 as the most *efficient* approach to schooling the young. In this model, a clear hierarchy exists, from the district superintendents at the top, through various district administrators, to the principal as a middle manager, and to teachers subjected to the principal's authority. Teachers concern themselves with instruction only but have no decision-making authority; they usually teach from curriculum materials adopted by the school board or the district office. There's little discussion of principals as instructional leaders; instead, teachers carry out instruction in isolated classrooms, in buildings sometimes described as "egg carton" schools, with two rows of independent classes on each floor and each teacher and class within its own protective compartment. Principals concentrate on the school's administrative tasks; their role in instruction is only to evaluate teachers for promotion and tenure (Cuban 1988). Most instruction is concerned with information transfer and the memorization of procedures, with little attention to conceptual development, independent thought, or what we would now call critical thinking; it is highly behaviorist in its assumptions and practices. (We assume that readers of this book are familiar with the language describing different approaches to instruction. Tool 1-B reviews these approaches, and the different ways they are described.) Observers from the 1890s until today describe these schools as intensely boring for most students, especially in high schools.

Traditional schools have coped with the increasing diversity of the student body—historically, with European immigrant children, working-class children coming to school (especially high school) in greater numbers, black migration from the South, and now many more Latino, Asian American, and other immigrant students as well as those with disabilities—by tracking them into different groups and teaching them differently. Tracking has been based on presumed vocational interests; on evidence of presumed "intelligence," measured in different ways; or on casual assessments of moral character and dedication (both likely ways for class and racial biases to creep in). Although tracking need not lead to lower levels of resources or a basic skills curriculum, in practice lower-track students have taken most of their classes with other lower-track students, rather than with peers with greater ambition and ability; they have usually faced watered-down curricula and lower demands, particularly in the so-called general track and in vocational coursework; and they have often been assigned inexperienced or poor-quality teachers. Tracking has almost inevitably worked to increase inequality among students as they progress from grade to grade—one of the many mechanisms underlying the dynamic inequality we examine in Chapter 6.

Most of these characteristics are still present in schools, especially urban schools. Many principals operate in hierarchical and authoritarian ways, with teachers playing little role in the decisions that most affect their classrooms. Despite new rhetoric about principals as "instructional leaders," there are still few consistent efforts to change the nature of instruction. Tracking still takes place, although the mechanisms may have changed; for example, though overtly vocational tracking in high schools has been reduced with the slow disappearance of traditional vocational education, other forms of tracking—like assignment to Advanced Placement, honors or college-bound tracks, and general tracks—accomplish the same separation of students. Efficiency is still the main criterion, and school performance is now measured by reading and math scores on standardized tests required by NCLB and state accountability measures. For those who believe in the power of threats, the NCLB standards and sanctions are the fullest expression of the efficiency movement that began around 1900. Most schools, and certainly most urban schools, follow many elements of the traditional approach, with some modifications around the edges—for example, some individual teachers use fewer behaviorist methods and more constructivist projects, group work, and conceptual approaches, mostly on their own.

In response to the dreariness and ineffectiveness of many traditional schools, a different approach to schooling has developed since the 1960s, and its proponents promise a greater variety of schools, greater effectiveness, equity, and innovation. The *entrepreneurial* approach encompasses choice and market-like mechanisms, including various voucher arrangements, small independent schools, and charter schools; they are often run on market-like principles—especially consumer (parental) choice, competition among alternative schools, and greater control of admissions and dismissal. By definition it's difficult to characterize this sector, because it encompasses the widest possible variety of approaches. Some entrepreneurial leaders have developed their own charter schools to establish schools that look like the collective schools we describe next, or that take particular approaches to equity (like Afrocentric or female-only schools), or that follow a particular philosophy (like Montessori schools or Multiple Intelligences schools). Others have deliberately re-created highly traditional schools (including military academies and back-to-basics schools) with traditional pedagogy, strict discipline, and authoritarian relationships. Still, a sector has now emerged with some distinctive contours. The rhetoric and pressure for entrepreneurial approaches appear to come not from idiosyncratic and innovative schools but from educational management organizations (EMOs) (these are conventionally capitalized in the literature) and charter management organizations (CMOs) with the capital, the private backing, and the institutional resources to operate chains of schools (Scott 2008). These relatively large organizations now include about one-quarter of all students in charter schools, though the numbers are elusive (Molnar et al. 2007).

In these chains, some distinctive features of the entrepreneurial sector become clearer. Principals largely act as managers and entrepreneurs rather than instructional leaders; in some cases they may have no background in education. They are responsible for getting new schools chartered, finding additional funding, hiring teachers, and making sure they implement conventional curricula. Teachers appear to be expendable in this process. With the expectation of "doing whatever it takes," teachers often have long work hours, as in the models of Teach for America and KIPP (Knowledge Is Power Program) schools, so teacher burnout and turnover are high. Teachers do not spend enough time in the profession to develop the expertise and innovative approaches required of other approaches. Outcomes are measured by conventional standardized test scores rather than by a broader range of assessments and outcomes. As a result, curricula are usually standardized and focused on tests, subjects are quite conventional, and pedagogy relies on behaviorist approaches and variants like Direct Instruction. Some EMO-run schools, like White Hat Management, use prepackaged curricula, requiring some teacher training in the use of these materials but no real professional development—that is, no real ability to teach in different ways according to students' strengths and interests.

The entrepreneurial sector has been largely dismissive of teacher unions, opting instead for more control of teachers through requirements for long working hours. Many organizations hire teachers without any credentials and then provide minimal amounts of training—Teach for America is the clearest example—rather than the years of professional development necessary to develop sophisticated teacher capacities. Some CMOs and EMOs pay relatively low salaries, particularly because high turnover means they are paying the low salaries of beginning teachers, not the higher salaries of experienced teachers. Thus, the opportunities for profit seem to come largely from teachers, who are (as in the usual corporate practice) workers to be exploited, not professionals whose development is vital to the enterprise. In addition, EMO-managed schools tend to have fewer special education students and fewer low-income students than the surrounding district schools (Nelson, Muirt, and Meter 2001), suggesting that they make some effort to keep out high-cost students. In the end, the opportunities for profit in entrepreneurial schools arise from a conventional corporate strategy: keeping worker salaries and costs low.

Entrepreneurial schools' "solution" to student diversity is also different from that of traditional schools. Charter and choice schools require application, and so they are likely to attract parents who are most actively engaged in the education of their children; the mantra of choice becomes a substitute for conceptions of equity. In a market-like system, consumers/parents are responsible for making wise choices. If there are inequities in the ability to make choices, or inequalities in purchasing power, these are beyond the responsibility of suppliers/schools. These schools also have greater ability to dismiss students; as one teacher said, "We have ways of asking people not to come back. We really operate like a private school." Disruptive, troublesome, or low-performing students can thus be eliminated more easily than in public schools. If the entrepreneurial sector expanded substantially, a crucial equity question would be where to educate those rejected from the entrepreneurial system.

Although some communities strongly support schools that fall within the entrepreneurial sector, there's little evidence that they are superior, even in conventional terms. In a 2009 study of 70 percent of the nation's charter schools, 17 percent "provide superior education opportunities for their students, nearly half have results that are no different from the local school options, and over a third, 37 percent, deliver learning results that are significantly worse than their students would have realized had they remained in traditional public schools" (Center for Research on Education Outcomes 2009, p. 1). Elementary schools scored better than middle and high schools, but students in charter high schools had "significantly worse results." More alarming for equity are the results for black and Hispanic students, where the "learning gains are significantly worse than those of their traditional school twins" (p. 6). So the notion that choice leads to superior schools just isn't right. Our working hypothesis is that to be successful *and* equitable, entrepreneurial schools need to have the same conditions as the schools we describe as collective, and when they do not—when they use inexperienced teachers, routine teaching, and principals as managers rather than instructional leaders—they simply replicate the conditions of traditional schools.

Proponents of school choice and vouchers have often portrayed their approach as the only alternative to low-quality traditional schools. However, in the past decade or two a very different approach has developed. We call these *collective schools*, or sometimes collaborative schools, because the entire school—teachers, administrators, students, parents, and staff—participate in determining the direction of the school, including its instruction, its equity practices, and its change practices. Collective schools engage in collaboration among teachers, of course, but collaboration is not unique to these schools. In other kinds of schools it often takes place in much more restricted forms; for example, when English

Key concept
collective
schools

and history teachers collaborate about their subjects, or second-grade teachers collaborate over the consistency of instruction. Similarly, collective schools should be cohesive, but both traditional and entrepreneurial schools can be cohesive even though they follow a very different philosophy of education. The term *collective* implies a joint and equal responsibility because the people in them are connected to each other and to a vision for change. The collectives that emerged from the many social justice movements of the mid-1900s were committed to collaboration and much more; they were also committed to exercising political and social power in particular arenas, just as we envision that teachers in collective schools are committed to participation in government policy (the subject of Chapter 4), to school reform (Chapter 5), and to policies outside of education (Chapter 6). These collectives exemplify the need to combine theory, action, and reflection (Freire 1970); they are based on similar values, which in the case of schools include consensus on the centrality of instruction as well as a commitment to equity. But the commitment to equity is different and deeper than the commitment to equity promoted in both traditional and entrepreneurial models, which often take forms that lead to inequitable outcomes. Instead, collective schools are institutions in which individuals are willing to have conversations about race, class, privilege, and the joint responsibility of the teachers to work together for justice.

What we call collective or collaborative schools have been described in other ways: as schools in which the *internal accountability* of teachers and leaders to one another has allowed more cohesive responses to external accountability (Carnoy, Elmore, and Sisken 2003); as schools with *distributed leadership* (Spillane 2006; Spillane and Diamond 2007), where teachers as well as administrators play leadership roles in various decision-making committees and school-site councils; and as *professional learning communities* stressing collaborative decision-making by the community of teachers and leaders (DuFour, Eaker, and Karhanek 2004; Little 2006). These schools stress the effectiveness of instruction rather than efficiency in the traditional sense. They usually move toward more constructivist forms of teaching and learning and incorporate a great range of "higher-order" and "critical thinking" abilities and more project-based and authentic assessment. They place a greater emphasis on the ability of teachers to devise their own materials and curricula, to set standards among themselves, and to review student work not only as a way of ensuring consistency among teachers but also as a way of agreeing about appropriate content and standards. Schools with theme-based approaches, including high schools with theme-based pathways (Oakes and Saunders 2008), are more likely to be collective schools because both the vision of the school and the integration of coursework around a school's theme require collective direction. Collective schools demand more of teachers than do traditional schools, but in return they provide teachers with decisive roles in the improvement of the school and central roles in shaping instruction. To use the terms we explore in Chapter 2, they promote *professional* roles for teachers rather than the subordinate, isolated, and deprofessionalized roles in traditional schools, or the exploited and deprofessionalized roles in many entrepreneurial schools.

Collective schools also take a different approach to the diversity of students—one of several reasons why we think that only collective schools can be truly equitable. Rather than relegating low-performing students to programs or tracks with *fewer* resources, the dominant approach in collective schools is to allocate *more* resources to low-performing students, in an effort to improve their performance rather than to sort them out of mainstream educational experiences. Though we will discuss these resources further in Chapters 3 and 6, they include allocating the strongest rather than the weakest teachers to low-performing students; enhancing the constructivist or "balanced" forms of instruction that are particularly necessary for low-performing students, in place of the remedial pedagogies that are so often used elsewhere; creating high expectations for students through the collective decision-making of teachers; developing interventions that diagnose learning problems quickly and provide targeted solutions that return students to mainstream classes, rather than interventions that create permanent low-quality tracks; and worrying about a wide range of effective resources, including practices that support racial minority and immigrant students. The basic response of these collective schools to diversity and inequality is therefore totally different from that of either traditional or entrepreneurial schools.

Examples of collective schools have come out of the progressive school tradition that developed after 1900 and from the small school efforts of the 1980s to the present. Collective schools (or even collective subject-matter departments) often emerge when schools confront the reality of achievement gaps, or large numbers of students below basic and far below basic, and transform their organization and instruction with the understanding that traditional methods cannot possibly correct this problem. Some of their practices have now become common in the vast literature for educators: distributed leadership, the school as a professional learning community, principals and assistant principals as instructional leaders rather than administrators and managers, the need for higher expectations, and support for "higher-order skills" and "twenty-first-century skills" (all aspects of more conceptual and constructivist teaching) have become commonplace. But there's still more talk than action, more policy debate than classroom change, and that is why this book stresses the need for collective action on the part of everyone in schools as the only possibility for lasting change and durable outcomes for students.

For aspiring teachers, teacher-leaders, and others (like principals) who work closely with teachers, these three

dominant approaches clarify how different the roles of
teachers can be depending on what kind of school they
work in. The passive and isolated roles of teachers in the
traditional approach, the routinized and exploited roles
in the entrepreneurial approach, and the active and professional roles in the collective approach present very different images of teachers and their power. Although the
ability to create personal relationships with students and
with each other as teachers is possible in all three, the differences among them result not only from personal relationships but also from the institutional practices they
have adopted: how they define the roles of teachers and
reinforce that with hiring practices, professional development, and salaries; and how they define the roles of principals through the selection and preparation of leaders,
the control vested in principals, and the presence (or absence) of collective decision-making mechanisms like
school-site councils.

Focus point

As a result, *aspiring teachers, experienced teachers deciding where to teach, and teacher-leaders need to think about
the characteristics of the schools they want to work in.* Many
readers of this book may be working in traditional
schools but want to push their school in the direction of
collective responsibility; if so, understanding these practices is fundamental to making those changes. Others
may be in traditional schools and want to set up a charter
school or school-within-a-school, and understanding the
pressures on such schools may help avoid the pitfalls we
have outlined. Sometimes teachers and leaders in entrepreneurial schools come to understand the limitations of
the deprofessionalized approach and want to give their
teachers control over instruction, and here again understanding the differences among these approaches offers
educators ways to think about changes. So, as we stress
throughout this book, the choice among models or approaches to schools is not necessarily either/or, but most
likely both/and. Hybrid versions of these three models
are emerging; for example, charter schools may take ad-

vantage of parental choice by developing internally democratic or collective practices. In such hybrids, the teachers who assume leadership roles can develop ways of initiating change, as we stress particularly in Chapter 5. This quote from Margaret Mead is particularly apt: "Never doubt that a small group of thoughtful, committed people can change the world. Indeed, it is the only thing that ever has." This book addresses those who are willing to join the collective, and often messy and complex, struggle for just and equitable schools.

Despite the emphasis on the personal dimensions of teaching, teachers are never really alone, not even in the isolated classrooms of the traditional school. They are always influenced by forces from outside the classrooms. Some are obvious and burdensome (such as the requirements of NCLB); some are subtle and difficult to counter, like the differences in parental aspirations for children; and some of them are so tightly woven into the "grammar of schooling" that we can hardly think about the alternatives—for example, the practices of age-graded schools, or the inevitability of summer vacation rather than year-round schooling. Being aware of these forces is the first step in deciding which of them support teaching and learning, and which do not.

THE PURPOSES OF SCHOOLING

No matter how a school is organized and operated, it faces a number of decisions that must be made—if they are not made consciously, they will be made by default. One of these is the purpose of schooling, the goals of creating a specialized institution. Starting with a blank piece of paper, it's easy to come up with a long list of goals for education—some of them essential, and some quite marginal. In practice, however, a smaller set of goals has dominated. In many cultures and times, schools were initially created to teach children how to read—not to explore the wide expanse of literature available, but so they could read the great religious texts (the Bible, the Koran, or the Torah) and learn their lessons for appropriate behavior. Reading remains central, of course, but now secular purposes provide the rationale, through texts on history and social studies, biology and chemistry, auto repair and information technology (IT), and the kinds of critical and political perspectives that were never part of religious education.

When the movement for public schools began in the first part of the nineteenth century, their advocates called for *common* schools—for all children, with a common curriculum for all—to prepare citizens for their roles in a new democratic country. The conception of civic education justified the expansion of *public* schools for *public* goals. It also gave the public schools a role in moral education, because a dutiful citizen would obey the law, respect authority, and live by the codes of honesty, integrity, and personal responsibility. The legacy of the common school lives on, overtly in the social studies and history curricula, and in the broader idea that access to public schooling should be universal—whether for black students in formerly segregated schools, disabled students who used to be denied access, or immigrant students lacking support for learning a new language.

Another conception of schooling has stressed a *general* or well-rounded education, with students taught about the arts and humanities as well as "useful" subjects, about sports and sportsmanship, about new issues as they come to be important: fascism in the 1940s, globalization in the 1990s, environmentalism and global warming in the twenty-first century. Some schools have followed Howard Gardner's (1983) conception that there are "multiple intelligences," and these "MI schools" have tried to incorporate as many of these competencies into the curriculum as possible, rather than following the conventional emphasis on verbal and math skills only.

The increasing domination of occupational preparation in schools and colleges has made formal schooling and increasing education levels more important, but in many ways it has also pushed aside the civic and moral purposes, as well as the purely intellectual goals that had once been part of schooling (Grubb and Lazerson 2004). The signs of this domination are all around: in a raft of commission reports calling for strengthening the schools to remain internationally competitive, rather than to strengthen democratic institutions; in students who care more about accumulating credits and advancing to the next level of education in order to get better jobs than about learning; in the domination of colleges by vocational (or professional) majors like business, health occupations, and IT; and in the rhetoric of College for All and the college prep curriculum, with its promise that college will guarantee access to a middle-class life. To be sure, many elementary and middle schools have adopted themes (like the environment, the ocean, or another topic of interest to students) to organize the curriculum. Some high schools have organized themselves around multiple pathways or majors or subjects, some broadly occupational (business or health occupations) and some nonoccupational (like social justice or communications) to prepare students for more options than just going on to college (Oakes and Saunders 2008). In these cases schools modify the standard curriculum to incorporate other subjects, or goals such as "college *and* careers" rather than College for All. And, of course, the proliferation of charter schools has brought a much greater variety of purposes to education, even though most choice schools still have the goals of traditional schools.

In some ways, however, skills required for the twenty-first century are quite different from the ones demanded when the schools developed their current format for scheduling, courses, and requirements. An industrial economy dictated the ways schools organized themselves by bells, with short periods in high schools and then junior high or middle schools. The rows of desks and the rigidity of rote learning were preparing most students for the routine jobs of an industrial economy and for a dutiful and obedient citizenry. But in a postindustrial era some of those competencies are no longer as valuable. A set of "twenty-first-century skills" has been widely proclaimed as better suited to the modern workforce and modern politics, including such capacities as problem-formulation and problem-solving, more complex forms of communication, the ability to work in groups and across boundaries rather than as individuals, and taking responsibility for one's own learning and team results. The need to shift to twenty-first-century capacities, in schools still organized in nineteenth-century forms, is one of several reasons for our emphasis on shifting from traditional schools to collective schools.

More recent state and federal accountability demands have added their own contrary pressures. As many have noted, the development of high-stakes exams covering reading and math only—the two most useful subjects of the curriculum, presumably—has resulted in substantially reduced emphasis on other subjects, such as science and history as well as art and music, as if civic education and the humanities can be dispensed with. So we can see "basic" schools (especially some traditional schools) co-existing with schools with a much wider array of subjects and purposes.

This vast array of options about the purposes of schooling, and therefore about the curriculum, implies that within limits such purposes of education can be modified by teachers working individually and collectively. If students have overly utilitarian views of schooling as economic but not civic preparation, teachers working together can first recognize the problem and then collectively convince students of the value of broader perspectives. If assessments have overemphasized reading and math, teachers can work together to maintain other subjects in the curriculum, and operate politically—for example, through joining unions and taking positions on assessment—to broaden the curriculum. Developing theme-based approaches in elementary and middle schools, and theme-oriented pathways (or majors, or academies) in high school, requires the active participation of teachers. Many innovations need teachers who can *develop* curricula and assessments, rather than merely *administer* a test or textbook, and curriculum development is rightly part of the role of teachers as professionals (as we discuss in the next chapter). For teachers, there are substantial professional rewards when they participate in developing schools closer to their own ideals rather than living with goals brought in from elsewhere.

EQUITY AND INEQUALITY

The very idea of public schools in this country was based on equity as much as on civic goals. Tax-supported schools would be available to all children, including the poor, who would otherwise not be able to pay tuition. (Not surprisingly, this ideal was never fully met because of the early exclusion of black slave children and Native Americans, though a number of free blacks were able to send their children to public schools.) Horace Mann, one of the earliest and fiercest promoters of public schools, called public education "beyond all other devices of human origin, the great equalizer of the conditions of men [and women], the balance-wheel of the social machinery," and argued that the inclusion of all children in one system would create this "equalizer." Furthermore, the creation of public schools moved decisions about education from private hands into the public sector. There, democratic (and potentially equitable) decisions could be made not only about the purposes of education but also about conditions of access, funding, and resources (the subject of Chapter 3). The notion that schools should be the central institution ensuring equity in our society has been reinforced ever since, especially in the 1960s during the Great Society and more recently with discussions about eliminating the achievement gap.

But it quickly became apparent that the equitable ideals of the common schools had to contend with many other contrary pressures. One set of factors is rooted in the families and communities that students came from. Generations of educators have seen that middle-class and working-class students come to school with different levels of preparation for school—different vocabularies, different familiarity with letters and numbers and the other building blocks of reading and math, different attitudes toward teachers and schoolwork, different levels of background knowledge on which to build new knowledge. Virtually every statistical analysis of achievement has found that family background matters a great deal, no matter how it is measured (Sirin 2005), and many qualitative studies have confirmed the deeply rooted ways that parents of different class backgrounds prepare their children for school and continue to sustain their children's progress through schooling (Heath 1983; Lareau 2003). These are unpleasant facts, particularly in the United States, which has more inequality than most other developed countries, but ignoring them only ensures that their effects persist. Tool 1-C illustrates the inequalities in both earnings and the learning of the adult population, both much higher than in other developed countries that we like to compare ourselves to. Teachers and leaders might reflect on what it means to be an educator in a country of such high inequality.

The ways in which public schools have reacted to the diversity of students have mattered a great deal, particularly in a country with so many kinds of diversity—racial and ethnic diversity, to be sure, but also occupational diversity, income differences, diversity in family structures, variation from urban to suburban to rural, variation in the sizes and locations of communities, and diversity of life stages (Katz and Stern 2006). Around 1900, the common school formulation of equity—equal access and the same curriculum for all students—was replaced with the slippery notion of equality of *opportunity*. Equity changed from providing the *same* education to providing a *differ-*

ent education appropriate for students with different goals, depending on their "evident and probable destinies": the academic track for middle-class students "bound for college and professional and managerial work," industrial education for working-class boys likely to end up in factories, commercial education for working-class girls heading for clerical positions, the general track for individuals bound for unskilled work, and home economics for homemakers (Lynd and Lynd 1929). Other forms of differentiation followed, each of them premised on equality of opportunity: ability grouping, eventually based on testing; special classes for the "feeble-minded," the disabled, and immigrants; and the school segregation that followed residential segregation, with working-class and black (and now Latino) students concentrated in urban schools while white and middle-class students dominate the suburbs. These patterns, recognizing differences among students and then relegating lower-performing students to tracks with lower expectations and fewer resources, have persisted to this day.

Many other practices have contributed to inequality in schooling. Even though the common schools assumed access by all children, current advocates have identified and then worked to correct unequal access—among black students in segregated schools, among English learners without access to ways of learning English, and among students with disabilities. Public funding seemed more equitable than private funding of schooling, but around 1900, educators discovered that public funds depend greatly on the wealth of the local community (and the wealth of states as well). Ever since, the variation in funding among schools and among districts within states has come under attack by lawyers and advocates for low-spending districts. The requirement in No Child Left Behind to have "highly qualified teachers" in every classroom has clarified that working-class students and students of color are much more likely to have inexperienced teachers, those with emergency credentials, and teachers teaching outside their field of preparation. With the expanded conception of resources that we develop in Chapter 3, it turns out that expenditure per student, the target of so much litigation, is actually one of the most equally distributed resources (though it's still quite unequal) and that many other resources affecting learning and progress through school are more unequally distributed.

Given the many sources of inequality embedded in school practices and policies, it's not surprising that the outcomes of schooling in this country are so unequal—as measured, for example, by the high dropout rate from high school (between 25 and 30 percent, and much higher for students of color) and the substantial variation in test scores. The top students in this country are bound for the best universities in the world, while some of their peers still read at elementary school levels. Again, Tool 1-C illustrates that inequality in learning in the U.S. is higher than in the developed countries we usually compared ourselves to.

For educators who believe in social justice, the sources of inequality in schooling outcomes present powerful challenges. On the one hand, teachers and leaders who want to confront these forms of inequality must first acknowledge them, and then determine ways to counteract them—ways that we review in Chapters 3, 5, and 6. On the other hand, emphasizing the family and community causes of low school performance risks labeling low-performing students as hopeless or uneducable. Too often educators have blamed low performance on the chaotic conditions of family life rather than investigating whether school practices, or school reactions to family background, are also responsible. So *working for social justice involves walking a narrow line, diagnosing when school performance is in part due to the effects of family background, but never using that as an excuse to do nothing. In fact, it is the very reason to do more.*

Focus point

The inequities that stem from school practices are difficult to confront in other ways. Teachers can, of course, work on their own to enhance their relations with students, especially students of color, and to make sure that their treatment of students is evenhanded. But many inequitable school practices are outside the power of individual teachers to change, and they instead require collective action within a school—for example, to change school climate, to eliminate covert tracking, or to improve the quality of instruction. Sometimes reforms require district or state action, such as allocating teachers among schools in different ways, developing more powerful ways of preparing teacher-leaders and school leaders, or allocating funding and resources among schools and districts in more equitable ways. And sometimes inequalities within schools can be addressed only by focusing on noneducation policies—for health, housing, income support, or community development, for example—a topic to which we turn in Chapter 6.

In the end, schools cannot become more equitable without the hard work of teachers. Only they can develop the balanced approaches to teaching that seem most powerful (see Tool 1-B); only they can come to know their students well and learn to teach different students in different ways. When we look beyond the classroom—in examining alternative models of schools as we did earlier in this chapter, or district and state policies in Chapter 4, or school reform in Chapter 5—our recommendations are designed to develop supportive environments for teachers so they can act as effectively and equitably as possible. Simultaneously, that will enable teachers to see what they can expect from their schools, their districts, and their states.

THE ISSUES FOR THIS BOOK

In this chapter we have argued that the conception of a "teacher" varies a great deal. Certainly the responsibilities of teachers in traditional schools, entrepreneurial schools, and collective schools are quite different. In

Chapter 2 we continue to elaborate the potential roles of teachers, emphasizing again that more effective and equitable approaches to schooling require teachers to work in new ways—more collaboratively, with collective responsibility for outcomes; more engaged in the roles that teacher-leaders take on; more professional, in the ways that professionalism has traditionally been defined in this country. We also confront the nature of unionism, partly because unions provide many teachers with a sense of identity as well as ways to engage in collective action, but also because teacher unions have often been blamed for the rigidities and inequities of schools. Teachers need to understand why this sometimes happens and what can be done to make teacher unions themselves part of the movement for school reform and social justice.

Many issues in schools and school reform, and particularly the inequalities caused by schools themselves, involve resources—of which money is the most obvious. Teachers and teacher-leaders who want to participate in making their school more effective for students, as well as more equitable, therefore need to understand the variety of resources in schools and which ones are most effective. In addition, the relationship between money and resources has been a tricky and contentious issue. The simple idea embedded in the Money Myth—that improving schools inevitably costs more money—proves not to be true (Grubb 2009). Even when schools have plenty of money, as a few private and public schools do, there prove to be many effective resources that cannot be bought, so more money provides little advantage. In times and places where school funding is tight, such as the current recession, it's imperative that educators understand what resources can be developed *without* spending a great deal of money. Chapter 3 will therefore examine the conventional and alternative conceptions of money and the resources it can only sometimes buy, stressing the roles teachers play in making resource decisions.

As we have already clarified, many influences on schools and classrooms come from outside the school—from district, state, and federal policies, and often from shifts in public thinking about schools that are expressed in commission reports. Teachers need to know about policy-making at these levels if they are to understand the influences on their own classrooms and schools, the subject of Chapter 4. In addition, teachers can be political activists, especially through their unions and sometimes through disciplinary groups (like the National Associations of Teachers of Math and English). We also outline in that chapter what teachers might expect (or demand) from district, state, and federal policymakers that would support their own efforts to create more effective and equitable schools.

Ever since *A Nation at Risk* was published in 1983, policy-making has focused on reforming schools in various ways: to develop higher standards; to make schools more equitable, now described in the goal of eliminating the achievement gap; or to provide parents and students with more choices, particularly in entrepreneurial approaches. Teachers play central roles in all these reforms, though teachers have often grown weary of reform after reform, and critics often blame teachers for resisting change. Chapter 5 examines the recent history of reforms and potential roles of teachers. In particular, we consider what useful approaches to reform look like, what kinds of evidence they require, and what can be done to make reforms permanent rather than ephemeral. In the end, it is the relationships among teachers and their leaders, within the institutional context, that count most in furthering a reform agenda. Without adult collaboration and appropriate interdependence, schools do not change or reform.

Chapter 6 draws together a number of issues developed in prior chapters about equity and social justice in education. Many of them are about distributive justice, or equity in the allocation of money, school resources, or outcomes. Another kind of justice involves procedural justice, the issues of fairness embedded in school procedures, including such tinderbox issues as discipline and student rights. The chapter also raises another kind of inequality and potential equity: the problem of dynamic inequality, or the inequality among students that develops and appears to become worse over the many years of schooling.

Finally, as we have already pointed out, some of the inequalities in education come from differences among families and communities—in incomes, access to health care and housing, in neighborhood characteristics like healthy rather than dilapidated conditions and crime rates. These are the result of social policies outside of education, though such policies have powerful influences on schooling and should therefore be seen as complementary to schooling. In the end, then, achieving social justice requires developing *both* educational policies *and* related social policies—both/and, not either/or, as John Dewey might say. Although this is a huge topic, Chapter 6 introduces some ways to think about the nonschool policies related to equity.

The possibilities of building new kinds of schools, with greater attention to instructional quality and to equity, with expanded teacher roles in both improving instruction and school decision-making, and with a more participatory approach to leadership, present teachers with a kind of trade-off. On the one hand, the new roles for teachers in new kinds of schools require a different kind of teacher, as we clarify in Chapter 2. These roles require both thinking outside the classroom and more work participating in activities outside the classroom. But this shift provides the opportunity for teachers to become real professionals, with the kind of knowledge and autonomy that other professionals enjoy, and to create the conditions of work that are more participatory and gratifying. In the end, we will argue, this is one of the only ways to make schools more effective as well as more equitable.

DISCUSSION QUESTIONS

1. Think about who or what groups make the important decisions in your school—decisions about the curriculum, about money and resources, about hiring and firing, about discipline and other procedural issues. How do teachers participate in these decisions? Would you say that decision-making is concentrated in the hands of the principal and a few others, or is it *distributed* widely among members of the school community—or does it follow some other pattern?

2. What are your own roles outside of the classroom—as members on various school committees including grade-level committees, as members of small learning communities, as coaches or mentors to newer teachers?

3. Tool 1-B provides an introduction to different approaches to instruction, an enormously complex subject that is usually part of teacher preparation programs. Use this tool to understand both your own teaching approaches and the approaches that dominate in your school.

4. When teachers, assistant principals, and the principal in your school discuss students, how do they describe them? By their individual likes and dislikes, strengths and weaknesses, and approaches to learning? By the characteristics of their families? Or by other characteristics?

FURTHER READING

Carnoy, Martin, Richard Elmore, and Leslie Siskin, eds. 2003. *The New Accountability: High Schools and High-Stakes Testing.* New York: Routledge.

Dewey, John. 1916. *Democracy and Education: An Introduction to the Philosophy of Education.* New York: Macmillan.

DuFour, Rebecca, Robert Eaker, and Gayle Karhanek. 2004. *Whatever It Takes: How Professional Learning Communities Respond When Kids Don't Learn.* Bloomington, IN: National Education Service.

Grubb, W. Norton, and Marvin Lazerson. 2004. *The Education Gospel: The Economic Roles of Schooling.* Cambridge, MA: Harvard University Press.

Spillane, James. 2006. *Distributed Leadership.* San Francisco: Jossey-Bass.

Spillane, James P., and John B. Diamond, eds. 2007. *Distributed Leadership in Practice.* New York: Teachers College Press.

TOOL 1-A: "WE LIVE THROUGH INSTITUTIONS"

Read the quote below from Bellah and colleagues, highlighting words and phrases that are of particular importance to you. Then engage in a "popcorn" or "shout-out" read-aloud, where participants say the words or phrases meaningful to them. Repetition is fine. Then discuss in trios the role of the personal and the individual in the school as an institution. Talk about other institutions of which the participants are a part and how their roles and responsibilities in schools and in those institutions are the same or different.

> One of the greatest challenges, especially for individualistic Americans, is to understand what institutions are—how we form them and how in turn they form us—and to imagine that we can actually alter them for the better. . . . As we showed in *Habits of the Heart*, Americans often think of individuals pitted against institutions. It is hard for us to think of institutions as affording the necessary context within which we become individuals; of institutions not just restraining but enabling us; of institutions not as an arena of hostility within which our character is tested but an indispensable source from which character is formed. This is in part because some of our institutions have indeed grown out of control, and beyond our comprehension. But the answer is to change them, for it is illusory to imagine that we can escape them. (Robert Bellah et al., *The Good Society* New York: Knopf, 1991, introduction, "We Live Through Institutions," 5–6.)

TOOL 1-B: UNDERSTANDING APPROACHES TO INSTRUCTION

In the chart below, list five practices or activities from your classroom practice in the left-hand column. Then read the short description in Section I of different approaches to learning and instruction. (This is a highly abbreviated form of learning theory and teaching.) We stress that teaching and learning may not be "either/or," either behaviorist or constructivist, but "both/and" or balanced, as teachers choose appropriate strategies for teaching because they understand how learning takes place and what might enhance learning. Identify your practice as mostly behaviorist, mostly constructivist, or balanced.

Take one example and discuss with a partner (about 5 minutes per person). Then take another example that is either mostly behaviorist or mostly constructivist. How would you change it to be more balanced?

Then read Section II below. How does this help inform you about your teaching?

Classroom Practice	"Name"	Analysis of Teaching Is the practice mostly:
Example: demonstration of dividing fractions	Direct instruction	___behaviorist, based on information processing and transfer? ___constructivist, based on conceptual understanding and making meaning as a result of experiences? ___balanced?
		___behaviorist, based on information processing and transfer? ___constructivist, based on conceptual understanding and making meaning as a result of experiences? ___balanced?
		___behaviorist, based on information processing and transfer? ___constructivist, based on conceptual understanding and making meaning as a result of experiences? ___balanced?
		___ behaviorist, based on information processing and transfer? ___constructivist, based on conceptual understanding and making meaning as a result of experiences? ___ balanced?
		___behaviorist, based on information processing and transfer? ___constructivist, based on conceptual understanding and making meaning as a result of experiences? ___ balanced?
		___ behaviorist, based on information processing and transfer? ___constructivist, based on conceptual understanding and making meaning as a result of experiences? ___balanced?

A basic dichotomy in approaches to teaching can be expressed in many different ways. One approach concentrates on transferring information from teacher (or textbook) to students, or demonstrating particular procedures (like long division, or the "formula" for the five-paragraph essay). There is usually one way to do something, and repetition is used to reinforce learning and make sure it transfers to long-term memory and then to other tasks. This approach focuses on part to whole instruction (learning parts of a complex competence, like learning spelling and grammar before attempting any writing), on lecture and other teacher-dominated forms of instruction, and on drill and repetition. It may include such things as mnemonic devices and other ways of encouraging memory. This approach is sometimes called Direct Instruction, or traditional instruction, or behaviorist teaching (referring to learning in response to rewards and punishments); in its worst forms, it is criticized as "drill and kill" or "skills and drills." Scripted curricula are extreme forms of this pedagogy, and "remedial" pedagogy—drill and practice on basic skills—also illustrates this approach. This approach often ignores the students' level of cognitive development, because some students may not have mastered what is considered a basic concept or skill but have moved on to more sophisticated cognitive processing.

The opposite approach is usually referred to as constructivist teaching, or teaching for conceptual understanding, or teaching for meaning, or the inquiry approach to teaching, or progressive or innovative teaching. It stresses understanding the purpose of a complex competence (reading, or writing, or long division) before drilling on the details. It proceeds by whole to part instruction, and uses much more student-centered methods, including discussion, student-initiated topics, and projects; it is based on constructivist learning theory, which promotes dialogue between and among peers as an essential part of helping students construct their own understandings of concepts, procedures, and meanings. It is also called *student-centered* rather than teacher-centered because students are active participants in their own learning rather than passive recipients ("blank slates" or "empty vessels") of teacher-generated knowledge. There are many other ways that educators and researchers express these differences, however, and curriculum materials, textbooks, and computer-assisted instruction are not always explicit about their pedagogies, so teachers need to be careful in understanding which approach is embedded in teaching materials.

Although a dichotomy between these two approaches has been discussed by many educators, many teachers understand the need to draw from both approaches—often called *balanced instruction* or *hybrid instruction*. There's no recipe for balanced instruction, so an appropriate combination of information transfer and conceptual approaches is part of the art and craft of teaching.

What evidence is there that constructivist or balanced instruction is more effective? This has been the subject of the "reading wars" and the "math wars," where a great deal of anecdote and armchair theorizing have taken the place of evidence. There are, however, at least three kinds of evidence. One is that some statistical analyses have shown more constructivist or balanced instruction to lead to improved learning. For example, Michael Knapp and Associates (1995) showed that low-income students performed better in classrooms with more practices following "teaching for meaning" rather than conventional instruction. W. Norton Grubb (2009) used a rich data set to show that teachers who reported more innovative and conceptual practices generated higher test scores for their students; a few other studies have used the same data to support similar findings. A second kind of evidence comes from evaluations of large-scale education reforms. These have generally found that the only reforms to enhance test scores adopted special approaches to instruction using conceptual or inquiry-based approaches, while other reforms paying little attention to instruction may enhance motivation and progress through schooling but not measures of learning (e.g., Quint 2006). Finally, the National Research Council has summarized the vast literature on instruction in reading (Snow, Burns, and Griffin 1998); on adult learning (Bransford, Brown, and Cocking 1999); on teaching math, science, and history to students (Donovan and Bransford 2005); and on motivation and engagement in high schools (National Research Council 2004). All of these support the idea that effective instruction should draw from both constructivist and information-processing theories.

TOOL I-C: INEQUALITY IN EARNINGS AND LEARNING IN THE UNITED STATES

Figure 1.1 identifies the inequality in earnings, as measured by the Gini coefficient (a measure ranging from 0, perfect equality, to 1, perfect *in*equality) on the y-axis, compared with the inequality of learning in the adult population, measured by the variation in reading test scores from the International Adult Literacy Survey. The United States ranks highest in both kinds of inequality; the other English-speaking countries are also high on both; and the Scandinavian countries are relatively more equal. Similar results exist for math. Though the underlying causes of inequality are complex, teachers and leaders might reflect on possible causes and on what it means to be an educator in a country with such high levels of inequality.

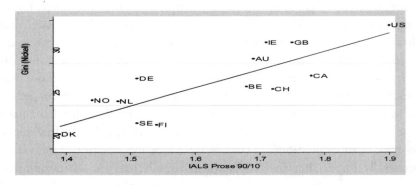

Figure 1.1.

Source: Grubb (2009), figure 1.1, based on data in Nickell (2004), table 9, from the Luxembourg Income Study for earnings and from the International Adult Literacy Survey for prose literacy.

CHAPTER TWO

THINKING ABOUT TEACHER LEADERSHIP

New Roles and Responsibilities in Collective Schools

A
S WE DESCRIBED in the previous chapter, the traditional school, with its hierarchical authority and compartmentalized (or "egg carton") classrooms, too often limits how teachers, leaders, and districts interact and how students learn. Because a fundamental requirement for workplaces (including schools) in the twenty-first century is the ability of all participants to work together, classrooms and schools function better as collectives. In this way, teachers and schools can simultaneously improve meaningful learning for students, reinforce the civic role of schooling, and model the twenty-first-century workplace. To accomplish this, teachers in the collective or collaborative school can be instructional leaders for student learning as well as engage in their own learning to improve their teaching and their schools. They should assume joint responsibility for professional development, because they themselves can better decide the ways in which to develop their own

capacities. Similarly, in assuming responsibility for student learning, they become responsible for the range of assessments and the roles assessment can play in student learning, not just in accountability to external requirements. By cultivating shared governance, they develop expanded roles as teachers in institutions that value democratic processes. Thus, in tandem with leaders who support new roles for teachers, they participate in institutional structures that better serve the demands of modern schools, workplaces, and democratic participation whether inside or outside the school.

In thinking about the new roles of teachers, it's crucial to remember the twin goals of schooling: academic achievement *and* the social development of youth are intertwined in the collective school. Virtually all teachers recognize the need for basic literacy and math proficiencies and, later on, science, history, other academic subjects, and then occupational competencies. But these conventional subjects are a small part of what is needed to educate the "whole child," to develop the norms and values necessary for many adult roles. These are often embedded not in explicit courses but in the "hidden curriculum"—the ways teachers and students interact with one another, the authority teachers have, the ways that students move from grade to grade and teacher to teacher, and the tendency to value certain subjects over others (Dreeben 1968). Indeed, the roles of teachers as experts (the "sage on the stage") in relation to subordinate students, in conventional "teacher-centered" instruction and traditional models of schooling, contain their own lessons about authority and expertise, just as student-centered instruction (and the teacher as "guide on the side"), with greater roles for student decisions and co-construction of knowledge, is more consistent with schooling for a democracy. These kinds of "lessons" take place all the time, whether schools intend them or not. Sometimes, as in the discipline issues we examine in Chapter 6, teacher-centered approaches create serious

Teachers have crucial roles to play in resource decisions.

problems, experienced by students as cases of procedural injustice. In many aspects of the school, then, the preponderance of certain teaching models—expository teaching and overuse of direct instruction to the near-exclusion of inquiry and problem-based learning—affects students and distorts the professional development of teachers in ways that are counterproductive to useful learning outcomes for both students and teachers.

An example clarifies how this unproductive approach impedes learning—including teacher learning. Teacher preparation days in August follow a typical script. Administrators throw up test scores on a screen using PowerPoint. In reviewing the data, a racial achievement gap is predictable. This is treated as a statement of fact rather than a learning opportunity to examine the causes of the "gaps" or to explore different courses of action. Teachers often feel accosted by the data, and, in self-defense, tend to shift blame onto the unequal economic system, onto families, or onto the inadequate test. The data are followed by traditional professional development (PD). Even if the leadership team planned and facilitated the PD, it is often a series of disconnected events that punctuate the school year, without clear planning or outcomes directed at improving teaching practice. These activities nearly always ignore the emotional content of the process—the sense of impotence and disappointment among teachers arising from test scores. This exercise is rarely used for problem-posing, teacher learning, or planning for those activities (including teacher-centered professional development) that might respond to the causes of achievement gaps and help teachers see themselves as problem-solvers and professionals. The end result includes demoralized and demeaned teachers, externalized blame, and ineffective responses to what is, after all, a serious school and social problem—the persistent achievement gaps in public schooling.

This scenario illustrates the chasm between how teachers experience the traditional model of schools and how administrators replicate a feeling of "us versus them" in this kind of organization. In a traditional school organization, it is difficult to rethink the roles of teachers and leaders in supporting common goals because both relationships and pedagogical approaches are locked into authoritarian ways. In the collective school, a new kind of teacher (as well as a new kind of leader) thinks and acts differently—"us *and* them," "both/and" (both teachers and administrators) instead of "us versus them" or "either/or." One antidote to the traditional isolated classroom involves peer observations so teachers can learn what happens in other classrooms. Administrators also have a better sense of teacher needs if they spend more time within classrooms, using observations as the content for professional development. This "both/and" approach is driven *both* by teachers who use instructional issues (including the achievement gap) as the basis for reflection, inquiry, professional development, and reform *and* by leaders promoting school practices that allow all teachers to participate in shaping school improvement.

Of course, there are substantial barriers to the teacher (and leader) roles we suggest in these collectively constructed schools. After all, the traditional approaches have been developing for two centuries at least, and multiple factors—school governance, teacher preparation, most principal preparation, district expectations, union contacts—have reinforced these roles. But there are other ways of doing things, and we focus the rest of this chapter on four areas that provide substantial leverage for changing the roles of teachers and leaders: (1) instructional leadership in and out of the classroom, (2) expanded forms of professional development, (3) collective accountability for student learning, and (4) varied and collaborative roles in governance structures.

New roles for teachers are crucial for effective schools, particularly for improving the quality of instruction and many other collective resources necessary for effective schools. In turn, effectiveness is a prerequisite for equity in education, because many of the urban schools where low-income students, students of color, and immigrant students are concentrated lack the conditions for effectiveness. But there is one additional role for teachers we examine: their role as advocates for social justice, and specifically as individuals willing to confront the inequities of class, race, and ethnicity in the United States—subjects that are among the most difficult to raise and resolve in all aspects of American life. We devote the last section of this chapter to exploring how schools can productively engage in these topics, to confront the enormous inequities associated with these differences both in and out of schools.

TEACHERS AS INSTRUCTIONAL LEADERS

We all recognize teachers as leaders in their own classrooms, although we are not often explicit about this formidable responsibility. Teachers spend most of their workdays in classrooms, and under most conditions we trust them to be instructors and role models for students. Although this has always been the case, recognizing this phenomenon as an organizational principle and a principle for more democratic and distributed leadership practices is not widespread. When we recognize teachers as instructional leaders in their own right, then we must acknowledge that leadership is already distributed in every school, even if its governance structure does not recognize that. Recognizing the existing leadership of teachers can have a multiplicative effect because with teachers as instructional leaders, a school has leadership with greater density—more leaders per school—and a higher degree of leadership, with more responsibility for each teacher. As teachers take on different roles, they develop a growing ability to lead and change schools—an effect we need in many underresourced schools, where human resources are the most fundamental requirement for powerful

Leadership is already distributed in every school, even if its governance structure does not recognize that.

change. (See Chapter 3 for discussion of fiscal and non-fiscal resources.)

Of course, some teachers are better prepared for certain types of instructional leadership than others. New teachers, for example, usually need to focus on developing their own teaching, and others types of leadership needed in the school may not be interesting to them. Some teachers may play the roles of engaged participants rather than leaders, but this may provide important forms of apprenticeship developing the teacher-leaders of the future. And principals must make some decisions, especially those that have to be made quickly, or that require the positional authority of the principal. Despite these caveats, the essential premise of teacher leadership should be clear: how teachers *both* work in their classrooms *and* learn through professional development should happen in collaborative ways, with greater teacher participation. This approach is generative, or constructed on the basis of teachers' needs and knowledge; it is dynamic rather than static, unfolding over time as conditions warrant; and it is multidimensional, rather than being confined to a single topic *du jour* chosen by others. Collaborative discussions of instruction and PD have the potential for stronger collective outcomes for adults and in turn lead to stronger outcomes for students. As James Spillane, Richard Halverson, and John Diamond (2000) suggest, this type of leadership develops through the *experience* of the organizational actors; it is influenced by the people and the processes they use to engage with one other. It is *constructed* by all the adults; it cannot be mandated by some adults or by outsiders. In this way, collaboration can generate collectivity from the inside out.

Teachers can then address a central area of professional concern: the level of authority they have over what they teach and how they teach it. The reservoir of craft knowledge that teachers have, and could share with their colleagues, can become the foundation of their professional development. By using critical friends protocols, teachers codevelop strategies that have the potential for influencing classroom practices and professional communities of practice. (See Tool 2-A for a Critical Friends consultancy and tuning protocol. We offer this as an example that has been successful in some schools, not as a prescription for practice.) In nearly every action research project of the teacher-leaders preparing to be administrators in the Principal Leadership Institute at UC Berkeley, the evidence from group inquiry is clear: given the opportunity to make strategic decisions about agendas, norms for meeting, classroom observation methods, and ways of discussing their own work and student work, teachers are willing to take the responsibility for self-improvement and continuous learning. But they do not do this overnight. Even while teachers ask for more autonomy, old structures die hard. Teachers need time to practice and to believe that their efforts will be respected by the "authorized" leadership; they do not immediately transfer their conversations about practice to classroom practice. Particularly if they have been working in a punitive accountability context, where teachers are punished for low student scores, they may be wary of taking professional risks by taking greater responsibility for student learning. However, these action research projects suggest that teacher-leaders can enhance student learning (as well as their own learning) through distributed leadership and by developing a richer portfolio of more consistent teaching practices. The teacher-generated methods and evidence from their practice promote learning at the same time they establish shared responsibility for outcomes.

Cross-Reference For more on teacher learning, see Book 1, Chapter 2.

In the process of letting teachers have more authority for decisions about their own learning, more structure paradoxically produces more freedom. By clearly delineating outcomes and learning tasks, protocols and procedures allow learners (in this case teachers) to learn instead of trying to figure out how to do something. Like a master class in theater, everyone learns from everyone else's work in this process. For example, the Critical

Friends protocol (Tool 2-A) offers one process for teachers engaging in thoughtful work together. The procedures for looking at student work are similar to cooperative learning methods or the formats for using culturally relevant pedagogy (LeMoine 2003) and for linguistically relevant practices (Dutro and Moran 2003): they all offer methods for teacher development that are immediately transferable to classroom use and can serve as the basis of further reflection and improvement. The procedures of the National School Reform Faculty (www.nsrf.org) offer still other guidance to teachers and leaders at many stages of development. Clear and consensual structures for adult interactions are balanced by the informal conversations that teachers have with each other in lounges, hallways, parking lots, and e-mail. Informal adult learning, including story-swapping (known to be a powerful source of change), is critical in the collective school, where consensus depends on resolving issues in small- and large-group discussions (Little 2006; Ball 1987). In the process, teachers as instructional leaders come to recognize these structures as important.

In effect, schools are places of both individual and collective action, as we discussed in Chapter 1. Richard Ingersoll (2003) argues in *Who Controls Teachers' Work?* that the most successful schools are hybrids of teacher autonomy and institutional structure. These schools promote teacher leadership by supporting (1) teacher autonomy over the areas of responsibility for which they are accountable— student achievement and the social development of children and youth, and also (2) the effective school (and district) practices that enhance such autonomy. Too little teacher autonomy supports forms of the traditional school; however, too much individual autonomy can lead to incoherent teaching practices across a school, which are detrimental to student outcomes. Instead, coherence across classrooms depends on practices and outcomes that are shared among all teachers (Elmore 2004) and requires far more interdependence among teachers.

The balance is tricky—many good intentions have been thwarted by abandoning structures and tools, ignoring the ways they foster relational trust (Kruse, Seashore Louis, and Bryk 1994). Adults sometimes balk at using protocols to support their own learning, thinking that they are artificial. Too often, teachers try something once and abandon it in their classroom or in their work altogether, ignoring research indicating that it takes six to eight tries before a practice becomes part of the pedagogical repertoire. Repeated efforts provide multiple ways to use the same protocol, treating it as flexible rather than fixed and rigid. Over the long run, adults who have control over their professional work, who make decisions based on collegial conversations, and who have some voice in professional development have higher levels of engagement in their work.

Classroom observations by peers and school administrators are key ways for improving as instructional leaders. Even though such observations are viewed in the conventional schools as intrusions into a teacher's autonomy, giving feedback about teaching is critical to developing collective responsibility for student outcomes. These observations promote teacher-to-teacher and teacher-to-leader conversations about instructional practice, and broader conversations about student learning and school culture. Like any other approach to adult learning, observations require a well-designed and strategic approach, with input from teachers and a consensus about how to observe, what evidence to look for, and how to talk to one another about the observations.

Frank Lyman, the originator of "think-pair-share," or TPS, developed an observational system that underscores the importance of TPS for adult learning: *We come to praise; we come to learn; we come to have conversations about practice.* From this perspective, adults look at each other's teaching to develop a common language around teaching and learning and to support each other in improving practice. A central principle of collaborative

We come to praise; we come to learn; we come to have conversations about practice.

inquiry about classroom practice is that observers should not rush to judgment. Because the purpose of observation is support, not evaluation and criticism, teachers can benefit from the observation process. Another component of useful observation systems—asking students about learning—can provide clues about learning we cannot get from watching teachers. All of these provide real-time and usable evidence for teacher conversations and teacher-leader discussions about improving instruction. They contrast sharply with judgmental teacher evaluation systems used by many districts, which can again lead to "threat rigidity" and turtle-like behavior rather than the reform generated by observations intended to improve practice. (See Toch 2008 for rethinking traditional evaluation systems to have more productive conversations about practice.)

The conversations that follow the observations are just as important. A consultancy protocol allows teachers to talk with each other about a particular issue, to take notes on feedback from discussants, and then to reflect on what was useful (see again the Critical Friends protocol in Tool 2-A). This results in an efficient process—each segment is timed—and one that is mutually beneficial, because one teacher's issue can help others. With clear protocols and agreements in place, teachers can pose and solve their own instructional dilemmas.

When teachers observe and improve learning collectively, principals and other school leaders play supporting roles. Although they may introduce decision-making structures and collaborative routines that facilitate such teacher conversations (Lemons, Luschel, and Siskin 2003), the decisions about how and when to use observation rest with teachers. These practices engender a greater sense of purpose, work satisfaction, and professional autonomy among teachers. Again, we stress that this does not happen automatically or quickly; it takes time for teachers to believe that "this time it will be different," and it takes a thoughtful process, examined iteratively to understand how to fine-tune the processes and protocols. But the result is that teachers acting collectively become instructional leaders in their own right, capable of improving the quality of teaching and learning, rather than simply managers of someone else's curriculum as in the traditional school.

TEACHERS' RESPONSIBILITIES FOR PROFESSIONAL DEVELOPMENT

The institutional design of the traditional school and classroom supported individualism, teacher privacy, and routine schedules. The very architecture of most schools reflects the independence of each classroom and teacher: teachers are often disconnected from each other and from leaders. This issue was not solved by the open-classroom design that came into use in the 1960s, for teachers and students who are more engaged are noisier and need enclosed spaces for learner-centered approaches. Instead of literally removing walls, sharing teaching practices requires that the walls be taken down figuratively, creating a classroom as a public space for engaging students in academic and social learning as well as a public space for teacher learning. This means that classrooms become more porous, as teachers and leaders observe other classrooms, breaking down the unproductive boundaries that exist in traditional schools.

In thinking about expanded roles for teachers, the balanced pedagogical approaches we outlined in Tool 1-B are equally useful for *student* and *adult* learning. Effective *adult* learning mirrors the attributes of effective *student* learning. This requires that learners (teachers as well as students) construct meaning for themselves and with each other as they engage in problem-posing and interactive problem-solving about teaching practices (Little 2006). We can call these practices "inside" or **teacher-generated forms of professional development**; they provide more participatory roles for teachers in diagnosing

Key concept
teacher-generated forms of professional development

and improving their teaching. This kind of learning is preferable to presentations from outside experts in which the teachers are passive rather than active learners.

An example of an "outside" workshop gone wrong is one developed for a school interested in launching professional learning communities (PLCs). The facilitator for the professional development session was told by administrators how resistant teachers were to the PLC concept. Recognizing the insider/outsider dynamic, the facilitator raised the conflict between the school's top-down decisions about PLCs and the teachers' autonomy and professionalism to signal her support for the contradictory roles of teachers (Ingersoll 2003). However, the teachers seemed surprised that teacher roles were framed in terms of this conflict and could not build on this insight. Although the assistant principal who organized the professional development session recognized that she needed to pay more attention to the teachers, she called the teachers resistant—she had an "us versus them" conception. But rather than being resistant, the teachers were hesitant to engage fully in professional development that felt imposed on them without a clear connection to their own concerns and needs. (We'll provide another example of such imposed professional development, about white privilege, in this chapter's final section.) A more thoughtful plan might have included teachers in choosing the subjects of professional development and developing different roles they could play with each other and with administrators. In this case, there could have been longer-run effects for school reform (discussed in Chapter 5) instead of a confrontation. Working from within a school and with teachers to determine changes would be more successful in engaging adults (Barth 1990; Little 2006) and a more useful way to build collective responsibility for outcomes.

Classroom observations that foster conversations about instruction therefore constitute a useful form of professional development, organized by "insiders," that reflects Roland Barth's (1990) contention that schools must improve from within. These and other practices described in this section redefine professional development: it is not a discrete event (like a onetime workshop or conference) but the everyday work of teachers thinking about how to improve teaching and learning, based on their own experiences and those of peers. Professional development is not an event but the daily and regular formal and informal work of teachers. Adults consistently report that their most useful learning is informal and often incidental, rather than formalized in afternoon workshops led by outsiders. They also report that enduring habits of mind and revised actions are often attached to rituals and routines that amplify their learning, including the stories that teachers tell one another.

Professional development is not an event but the daily and regular formal and informal work of teachers.

Storytelling is an ordinary but significant way for adults to share their work. By analyzing school stories and respecting the experiences of teachers who tell them, schools can emphasize reflection as a habit of mind. Teachers everywhere engage in story-swapping, but by putting some modest structures around the practice, it becomes possible to minimize "war stories," complaints that often lead to a downward spiral of griping. Teacher stories, carefully analyzed, then become a moving force for change. One element of the structure is a prompt, designed to elicit stories on particular themes; for example, a prompt might be related to a typical incident (a discipline case, for example) or a difficult decision. Then, by using a second structure—**reflective questioning**—in small groups, teachers listen to each other's stories, analyze them for general themes, and use them to make decisions about what to pursue in their collective practices. Such stories, accompanied by reflection and analysis, have multiple benefits: they provide information to individuals about the subconscious decisions they are making and the roles they are playing; they provide a self-generating needs assessment for structuring other teacher professional development; and they signal administrators about tensions and problems emerging among the faculty. Fred Brill (2009)

Key concept *reflective questioning*

illustrates the themes, reflective questions, and processes that are important for implementing storytelling.

Individuals or small groups of teachers can also enhance their professional knowledge by joining national and local organizations that promote deeper knowledge of subject matter or promote social justice. Membership in these organizations can contribute to the political organization and voice of teachers, as we discuss in Chapter 4, but they are first and foremost forms of professional development. Though individual teachers in more traditional schools may benefit individually from their membership, in a collective school, teachers share what they learn from conferences and publications through professional development and thereby magnify the individual benefits. Subject-matter organizations such as the NCTM and NCTE have counterparts in all content areas. They typically provide venues for exploring professional interests and sharing their expertise with colleagues, monthly or quarterly publications, instructional materials, and workshops and conferences that enable teachers to feel a part of a larger professional community. Social justice organizations, like Educators for Social Responsibility, Teaching for Change, Rethinking Schools, and the National Association of Multicultural Education, also offer personal and professional growth. They nurture a collective hope for different ways of teaching, leading, and organizing schools by connecting teachers to ideas and individuals who have been successful in creating collective schools or want to engage in doing so. Finally, local, state, and national nonprofits—for example, Solution Tree, the Association for Supervision and Curriculum Development, and the Hope Foundation—provide national conferences and materials to foster teacher professional development.

Thus, a menu of complementary professional development might include classroom observations by teachers as well as administrators; meetings facilitated by teachers to reflect on the results of observations; internal

Teacher stories, carefully analyzed, then become a moving force for change.

workshops teachers choose and lead; reflective story-telling, incorporating informal learning; occasional external workshops, chosen by teachers; and individual readings and attendance at workshops and conferences, where teachers who attend them return to share their learning with their colleagues. These are all ways to promote teacher professionalism and generate homegrown learning communities, in place of the one-shot workshops that often pass for professional development. Developing such "inside" forms of PD is not an easy task, after the isolation and bureaucratic responses of most conventional schools. But it is one worth pursuing because, in the end, adult ways of learning affect classroom practice and student learning.

TEACHERS' ROLES IN ACCOUNTABILITY

Recent assessment practices in this country have reinforced many patterns of traditional schools. As a result of state testing practices, NCLB testing mandates, and the sanctions that followed, several predictable organizational responses have taken place: "structures tighten; centralized control increases; conformity is stressed; accountability and efficiency measures are emphasized; and alternative or innovative thinking is discouraged" (Olsen and Sexton 2009, 15). As districts and states imposed curricular and pedagogical requirements with prescribed benchmarks and standardized exams, school-level administrators and teachers often complied because they felt they had no alternative if their students were to become proficient on state exams. NCLB shifted the focus from what teachers do to what students learn, but the narrow way that NCLB measures student achievement has not, in most schools, fostered productive discussions about student learning or the teacher learning needed to support students.

To accentuate the accountability dilemma, middle school and high school grading processes are often inconsistent within a single school. In one case, a high school assistant principal found that two teachers (out of 43) calculated their students' course grades by counting the final exam as 50 percent of the total, whereas others used homework for 20–50 percent of the grade and downplayed the final grade; in some cases (in violation of the state code), teachers were basing grades largely on attendance and tardiness. Without a clear message about what outcomes count for grades and what the role of learning is, some students cease trying—and are then labeled "apathetic" or "unmotivated" rather than confused by incoherent assessments.

Because conventional accountability has been so counterproductive, reasserting teachers' roles in assessment is a prime target for collective action. The collective school requires a more rigorous, consistent, and student-friendly approach to assessment. It demands that teachers and leaders understand assessment language and the assessment continuum, from formative to summative— the daily, weekly, quarterly, and benchmark assessments across a grade level, content area, or course level. Teachers can then engage in collectively developing assessments for grades or disciplinary areas. Together they examine student work using district or state standards-based rubrics, thereby fostering consistency in the signals they send students. This form of accountability further requires that students understand what it takes to become proficient on standards-based assessments, and that they have multiple chances to achieve the result. In one Georgia high school, for example, the grades are A, B, C, and "not yet," communicating by the assessment system the expectation of eventual success.

Under these conditions assessments become an intrinsic part of learning, and the assessments clarify to students what and why they should be learning—rather than serving only as exercises for ranking students and schools, with limited instructional benefit. This view reinforces teachers' roles in daily classroom assessments, the minute-to-minute checking for understanding that is the daily pulse of student learning and a primary part of the peer observations discussed earlier. When teachers reclaim assessment as a fundamental part of their professional work, and the conversations among teachers are focused on how to use assessments to guide their teaching, they develop more powerful roles in deciding what assessments can do. By augmenting daily assessments with the use of authentic summative assessments, like project-based learning, portfolios, and exhibitions, they send a message to each other and to students that learning is more than a year-end test. By taking leadership roles in the design and use of such assessments, they assume professional autonomy in new ways, and the "tools of their trade"—the assessments they develop collectively—become other ways of exercising leadership.

Unfortunately, the current pressure to use "engagement strategies" is often confused with activity-based teaching—teaching based on student activities but with no assessment of learning. Yet, if teachers concentrate their collaborative work on the connections between learning objectives and assessments linked to those objectives, pushing themselves to write objectives with observable assessments that are "student-friendly," they have a better chance of directing their daily teaching toward assessment. In fact, many of the strategies used for student engagement—like think-pair-share, equitable participation, and use of white boards—serve the function of daily assessment if teachers use them fully. Daily end-of-lesson assessments are critical and also serve multiple purposes. For example, a secondary teacher recognized that he was basing his teaching on activities rather than learning. By using an exit ticket, a task that asks students to respond to one or two questions to check for understanding, several results became evident. First, he began to stop about five minutes before the bell and focus on student reflection about their learning, fostering this kind of metacognition absent from most classrooms.

Second, taking time to have students put in their own words precisely what had happened in the class made the starting point for the next day clearer and solidified the learning for the day. He was able to use the exit tickets to make decisions about his teaching and the depth of student learning, and the reflection caused by the exit tickets meant that the learning lasted from one day to the next; both his teaching and student learning improved as a result. The use of a simple exit ticket doesn't seem particularly remarkable, but if teachers collectively focused on using this evidence to exchange ideas about improvement, this practice could foster the formal and informal learning we have discussed and provide the basis for professional development.

What about the highest-stakes accountability, the summative state tests that in turn are used for No Child Left Behind? Many of the curricular changes and assessments imposed on schools have been driven by these tests, on the assumption that "teaching to the tests" in large and small ways is the best way to enhance test scores. But some evidence suggests that this is a misguided way of bringing students to proficiency. With a rich data set from Chicago, Frank Newmann, Anthony Bryk, and Jenny Nagoaka (2001) analyzed the results of teaching math and writing in grades 3, 6, and 8. Students who received assignments requiring more challenging intellectual work—work that required higher-order thinking, in-depth understanding, elaborated communication, and connections to students' lives beyond school—also made greater gains in math and reading on the Iowa Tests of Basic Skills, a test that doesn't pretend to be multidimensional. They also had higher performance on the Illinois Goals Assessment Program, based on state standards. The implication is that students taught in more conceptual or constructivist ways do better on tests of basic skills, as well as on multidimensional tests that assess higher-order abilities. Conversely, the tendency to use remedial drill-and-practice pedagogy with low-performing students, in the hope that their scores on standardized tests will improve, often does not produce the intended results; many students remain in the low-performing category. Once again, if teachers engage more actively in assessment-driven instruction—in this case by developing both pedagogies and assessments appropriate for multidimensional teaching—they serve students more effectively.

Just as we reframed professional development as a teacher's ongoing responsibility, accountability is a daily responsibility. Like the professional development discussed earlier in the chapter, this is better accomplished in collaborative teacher groups than in isolated classrooms. Developing an assessment frame of mind, with a deep respect for daily assessment in improving teaching and learning, requires time, reflection, and co-planning—typically more time than teachers have. But if we want enhanced attention to learning and assessment, then schools and leaders need an imaginative approach to scheduling and teacher time. The master schedule, with opportunities for flexible grouping of students, common planning time (CPT), and professional development workshops, is a potential resource, and teacher-leaders should understand and participate in designing the schedule so that they can advocate for better ways to organize collaboration. This is becoming important even in elementary schools that need to reorganize for effective common planning time. There's no reason, for example, that the required instructional minutes should lead to the same unchanging daily schedule. Instead schedules can vary from day to day to allow for teacher collaboration, and grades (or subjects) could assess and regroup students in flexible classes and different sizes to meet student needs as long as they do not track them into classes for an entire year. In other education systems, such as those in Japan and China, teachers teach half a day and observe or collaborate the other half. This is not likely to occur in the United States, particularly as most U.S. schools are now suffering

If we want enhanced attention to learning and assessment, schools and leaders need an imaginative approach to scheduling and teacher time.

the effects of a fiscal recession. However, over the long run, teachers need to assert the value of time as a resource (to be further discussed in Chapter 3) and as a prerequisite for their engagement in assessment development and analysis. Accountability for student learning is the primary responsibility of teachers, and cohesive internal accountability practices, developed and monitored collectively, are powerful responses to external, top-down, and one-dimensional forms of accountability (Elmore 2004). To develop such responses, however, teachers must organize collectively to reassert their individual and shared responsibility in this domain of the profession.

TEACHER LEADERSHIP IN SCHOOL GOVERNANCE

As teachers broaden and deepen their collaboration with other adults and as leaders who fully support distributed leadership, they can take on a variety of governance responsibilities in the collective school. Engaging teachers requires breaking down another bureaucratic narrative: the "us versus them" presumption about the ways teachers and leaders operate in the traditional school. Too often teacher autonomy is framed as resistance or opposition to administrators, much the way teachers view students as antagonistic. Therefore, if adults expect to change the ways they collectively take responsibility for student outcomes, they, along with school administrators and districts, must rethink the nature of authority. Rather than viewing a difference of opinion as resistance, it can be recast as a productive ingredient of effective problem-solving, in which an ethic of listening to many voices is necessary for the most enduring solutions. This reframing is even more necessary if the work of teachers and leaders is to mirror democracy as a key goal of schooling.

Organizational participants who have been in competing roles instead of collaborative ones often have difficulty imagining another way. Schools can either be fortresses with drawbridges and the principal as king or queen, or they can consciously change the way they operate and welcome full participation of teachers and parents. The roles for teachers range from union representatives (discussed in Chapter 4), to participants on student study teams (SSTs) for students experiencing difficulties, to leading grade or department meetings. In high schools that have academies or schools within schools, teacher-leaders serve as heads of these small schools. Other roles for teachers are positions with more formal authority on leadership teams or serving on the school governance group that includes the administrators, parents, and teachers (called site councils in this section). The increased participation of teachers in school governance in turn has at least three consequences: greater participation in school micropolitics, the informal talk and decisions that are a part of any organization, and in productive responses to such politics; the participation of teachers in leadership roles that build their capacities; and the use of structures that support new organizational cultures.

There's no surprise here: adults talk to each other in formal and informal settings, and these conversations can either foster productive action or deteriorate into gripe sessions that contribute to a negative culture. These informal conversations, sometimes referred to as "micropolitical," take many forms and can be redirected: the gossip in the teachers' lounge or the parking lot, too often viewed as a negative element of organizational life, can instead be viewed as valuable problem-solving time. Faculty or department meetings, often times for complaining, can be reimagined and restructured, using appropriate agendas and protocols, to be more productive. These conversations in essence can pose problems that lead to problem-solving and decisions—*if* teachers and leaders are willing to listen to each other instead of responding by engaging in blame.

The effective school leader takes the pulse of the community by checking in regularly with teachers, but in a collective school it is the responsibility of teacher-leaders to generate input from all teachers and to bring those conversations into more formal governance—grade-level or department meetings or school-site councils. Input and information, often anecdotal, can become more systematic if teacher-leaders collect evidence for decisions from everyone, instead of relying on solutions that could be termed as "shooting from the hip." An example from a faculty meeting illustrates the difference: a problem was introduced and five persons complained, two repeatedly, giving the meeting a negative tone. The leadership team decided a survey would yield more complete evidence on which to base a decision. The survey evidence showed that the five complainers were a small if vocal minority; the other fifty-six teachers had useful ideas about how to proceed. Presenting the evidence at the next meeting resulted in more representative viewpoints and contributed to a more positive tone; the faculty was able to reach consensus about a school policy for the first time in three years. Teacher-leaders, who designed and analyzed the short survey with the principal's support, were central in reframing the conversation more productively.

Another criterion of shared governance, equitable participation—with an eye toward balancing the experience of veterans with the fresh ideas of novices—is sometimes tricky and requires awareness of competing interests and concerns. In some schools where teacher turnover is high, eager but inexperienced teachers without a complete sense of how schools operate often fill leadership roles. Though a fresh perspective is a much-needed ingredient of school governance, choosing less experienced teacher-leaders to fill governance roles could alienate veterans. Yet seniority is surely not the sole criterion for participation. In one middle school, a new principal determined that leadership team membership was inequitable: though over one-third of the faculty were people of color, only one person on the ten-member leadership team was Latino. The same pattern held true for the site council, in which a group of white parents overshadowed the majority Latino and African American parents. Thus, in addition to experience, a different standard for participation should be how well any governance structure represents student perspectives, needs, and outcomes rather than adult needs, desire for power, or convenience. An assistant principal termed one dilemma the "micro-macro conflict." As leader of a school within a comprehensive high school, she had to balance the micro interests of the small thematic school with the macro interests of the school as a whole. It may be hard to see the whole when a teacher is so deeply involved in one part, but cross-grade observations, visiting other grade-level meetings, and serving in leadership roles broaden those perspectives. Teachers who take up governance roles must be ready to negotiate the complex terrain of shared leadership, for maintaining an equilibrium among different points of view is the foundation of democracy.

To negotiate these complexities and avoid getting sucked into ineffective bureaucratic structures, useful antidotes include norms, agendas, protocols, and processes that support inclusion and shared voices. Valuable adult time is squandered when meetings are dominated by a long agenda with routine committee reports, unstructured participation that allows a few complainers to dominate the airspace, or quickly paced agendas that ignore deeper issues. In these cases, changing the discourse and participation patterns is vital. One format that makes this possible is **appreciative** or **constructivist listening**, described in Tool 2-C. At any meeting, there should be an opportunity to "check in" using a relevant prompt, take on leadership roles, and gain facility in working with other adults. This offers a generic protocol for developing a norm of listening to each other.

In the best situations, teachers engaged in leadership roles meet to develop common agreements about how to

Key concept
appreciative or constructivist listening

proceed, how to develop expertise in facilitation, and how to create time and space where they can bring up difficult issues. This process builds a professional learning community of teacher-leaders concerned about the direction of the school. Under these conditions, various adults take responsibility for student outcomes and then develop collaborative roles in the social development of youth—roles that they model when they work with other adults in these ways. Students know when adults are in sync and when they are not, and students can learn how to solve their issues collectively by seeing how the adults take care of governance. Through reinvigorated roles of teachers in the political life of the school, students can learn in multiple ways how to become active and socially concerned adults.

TEACHERS AS SOCIAL JUSTICE ADVOCATES

We have by now developed several roles of teachers as leaders in their classrooms and schools—as instructional leaders, as individuals constructing their own forms of professional development, as the stewards of accountability, and as participants in more democratic governance structures. All these roles are crucial for effectiveness, for without active teachers, schools cannot reform themselves. In turn, greater effectiveness is one of the most crucial equity policies, for ineffective schools cannot possibly help students—especially the low-income students, immigrant students, and students of color in urban districts. If schools are indeed to be "the great equalizer of the conditions of men, the balance wheel of the social machinery," as Horace Mann wrote in 1848, then all students—no matter their family background, class or race, zip code, or ethnic identity—must be able to rely on each teacher to make certain that they learn the academic and social content of a course of study.

As part of promoting equity and schools as the "great equalizer," teachers must also be advocates for social justice. This term has many meanings, but in our society—with its enormous differences of class, race, and ethnicity—one central element of social justice is advocacy for African American and Latino students, other students of color, low-income or working-class students, and immigrant students. They are the students who fare least well in schools; they are the victims of many different types of gaps, including the achievement gap; and they are all too often the victims of mistreatment, as we will argue further in Chapter 3. Therefore, teachers as advocates for social justice must become comfortable discussing issues of race, ethnicity, and class; diagnosing the issues underlying the "achievement gap"—almost always stated in racialized terms, as the black-white achievement gap, or white-Latino differences in graduation rates; coming up with solutions; and then putting those solutions firmly in place.

However, a dilemma emerges when teachers and schools—and sometimes districts—turn to the hard work of addressing racial and ethnic issues. There are many *practices* that have developed to make schools more supportive places for students of color—forms of culturally relevant pedagogy, the approaches associated with multicultural education (Gay 2000; Banks and Banks 2004), as well as more student-centered teaching that considers the backgrounds of all students and treats all students respectfully. However, though it is possible to introduce new practices like these, the ways teachers and schools do so are affected by their *beliefs*—belief that all students can learn versus the belief that some students are inevitably "behind" because of their race or class, belief in moderating the curriculum to support students versus the belief that all students should be taught the same academic content, belief in student-centered instruction rather than teacher- or textbook-centered teaching. Inevitably, beliefs influence school practices, and it's difficult simply to mimic certain practices without believing in them. In an ideal world, a balanced approach to this dilemma would

Cross-Reference
See Book 2 for the special role of school justice in ESL learning.

change *both* beliefs *and* practices, a "both/and" rather than an "either/or" solution (as we stress throughout this book). However, beliefs are often slower to change than instructional practices because they are more deeply rooted in our histories and our cultures—particularly in a society with deep racial and ethnic divisions, and with high levels of inequality (even though Americans often don't acknowledge these differences of class). This is why pushing teachers and leaders to change their beliefs prior to changing their practices, as many "diversity workshops" ask educators to do, sometimes results in teachers feeling threatened and then retreating, and in divisions among community members—black versus white, experienced versus inexperienced, academic teachers versus broadly occupational teachers—who need instead to be allies in advocating for students and families.

A specific example, in an elementary school with a small staff of fifteen teachers—fourteen of them white and one African American—clarifies the potential pitfalls. From the standpoint of the leadership team, teachers were not responsive to the students of color, who made up the entire student body (with 35 percent African American, 62 percent Latino, and 3 percent Asian). Two white teacher-leaders were self-proclaimed advocates for social justice, and they enlisted the support of the one African American teacher. They then formed a committee to address social justice and designed a survey to determine what teachers needed. The survey results indicated that teachers wanted more information and professional development about multicultural curricula—that is, instructional content and practices; they did not yet want to address their personal belief systems. Instead of responding to the teachers' stated goals and, by implication, their capacity for changing practice, the planning group decided to host an antiracism workshop led by two relatively inexperienced presenters. The workshop did not focus on multicultural literature or history, which could have been integrated into the curriculum and given teachers opportunities to learn more about the culture of their students, but instead asked teachers to examine white privilege—the special status white people have in a diverse but still racist society. The teachers were not prepared for that approach, had not requested it, and were surprised and upset. Most teachers felt they were being accused of being racists and folded their arms literally and figuratively; all forward movement in addressing the needs of students of color and multiculturalism stopped there. The "resolution" created unnecessary tension and divisions, and in response, all the planned workshops on this topic were dropped for the remainder of the year at the principal's direction. This is a perfect example of *threat rigidity,* which emerges if teachers feel attacked, causing them (in this case) to close down as surely as do rigid accountability requirements. The moral of the story, we think, is that approaches to social justice require care and creating a community of trusting individuals for the complex work of addressing both practices and beliefs.

Becoming comfortable discussing issues of race and class requires that adults have a clear sense of their own identities. As products of their histories, the individual identities of teachers inevitably influence the ways they relate to children and parents (Olsen 2008). Not every teacher has experience with the difficult examination of the self within the larger social system, even if all teachers want to teach students equitably. Many efforts to engage people in this conversation, including the poorly run diversity workshop just mentioned, are counterproductive because the level of discomfort that some teachers experience prevents them from engagement and change. Having "courageous conversations" about race or developing cultural competence—a deeper understanding of the norms of other classes and races—is too difficult a task to relegate to a one-day "diversity workshop." This is particularly true if these conversations concentrate on white privilege, contribute to the discomfort of white individuals, and virtually ignore the different needs of educators of color.

Furthermore, discussing racial and class privilege as individual characteristics rather than the structural characteristics of our society, not only may have unproductive results but also misses the opportunity to understand the deeper causes of racial and class differences (McIntosh 1988; Leonardo 2004).

**Cross-Reference
See Book 5,
Chapter 3 for a
discussion of
community
building in social
justice teaching.**

Examining identity as a basis for advocating social justice requires several steps. First, topics that touch personal and collective identity and history require norms of engagement, and the group needs to reach consensus on these norms. Second, the starting point for the conversation depends on the readiness of the individuals in each school, including knowledge of their histories and their individual and collective stories. One strategy that is particularly useful is developing understanding from personal narratives, thereby clarifying the continuum of beliefs and practices within a school. Relating these narratives also contributes to the community's collective story. There are many ways to do this, but one that has been successful for us is the use of the "I Am From" poem, an exercise in Linda Christensen's (2006) chapter in *Beyond Heroes and Holidays.* The point is to share personal histories in a format that is nonthreatening but leads to personal revelation. The exercise usually has the same result: it puts all participants on an equal footing in their ability to share their stories and identities, and it provides unexpected revelations about the histories of colleagues. With nonthreatening connections among members of a community, the relationships among teachers are strengthened, and the work of schooling children can be undertaken in unison.

Another exercise is the journey line, describing the roots of personal experiences over time (our journeys) that form our identities (see Tool 2-D). This strategy can be used for a variety of topics, including a professional development journey, a leadership journey, or a math or English journey. Sharing the important moments from our past that have influenced our present selves reveals the moving forces in our development, and then allows us to conceive of change in schools and society—parallel to changes in the self—before moving to practical applications. In using the journey line as the foundation for advocacy roles, teachers can gain a sense of individual and collective power and the ways they rely on each other. One variant is the "courage journey line," where participants think about the times they have mustered courage to do or say something they did not think they could do. A song by Holly Near, "Change of Heart," is helpful. It begins with the line "something changes in me when I witness someone's courage" and then shifts to children in ways that directly involve teachers: "do not forget the children . . . when their hearts are threatened." Every teacher has had a moment when he or she went to bat for a student; through these stories of courage, a community can share its commitment to courage. As with personal narratives, this is a nonthreatening and nonjudgmental way to share experiences because it relies on individual histories that become a part of the collective history of teachers in a particular school. It also offers a promising way to unify the *potential* community.

To some teachers who may consider themselves further along in their comfort with racial issues, this process may seem slow and incremental; they may be impatient to get on with the process of adopting new practices. However, it is counterproductive to have teachers "shut down" or go into their shells, and this brings all the important work of social justice to a halt. So we can only conclude that changing instructional practices related to children of color—in truth, like changing all instructional practices— requires slow but steady work, especially because beliefs in these areas are so deeply rooted. It has been our experience in doing this work with teacher-leaders preparing to be school leaders that finding the fulcrum in the beliefs/ practice continuum and calibrating carefully the readiness and capacity of a group to move forward have yielded strong results over time for those in our one-year program and been more effective for them as they move into leadership roles.

In this chapter we have described several roles for teachers: the role of instructional leader, that of fostering professional development as an internal process, the role of reasserting authority over accountability, the multiple roles of teacher-leaders in school governance, and the catalytic role of teachers in advocating for social justice. These roles are central to developing the collective school we have described; all are fundamental to improving instruction and developing the school reforms we outline in Chapter 5. All of them require teachers to consolidate their knowledge as insiders within schools, and to use it as a catalyst to move from the isolation of traditional classrooms to participation with other teachers and leaders in a community of practice. All of them require understanding that a school is not just a collection of wonderful people, charismatic teachers, and hero-principals. Instead, it is a collective institution with particular characteristics and practices, forged by the people within the institution, and with each individual realized only in and through community.

DISCUSSION QUESTIONS

1. What currently constitutes professional development in your school? What roles (if any) do teachers play in designing professional development, deciding on topics, or presenting to the school community? How would you characterize professional development: ongoing and continuous or individual workshops/activities disconnected from one another?

2. What kinds of informal professional development happen in your school? How could these be structured to be more coherent?

3. How have external exams, such as state accountability exams, influenced teachers and teaching in your school? Have the school's responses to these exams been determined by the school community, by the district, or by state mandates?

4. What roles do teachers hold in school governance—either advisory committees or decision-making committees in your school? What kinds of committees have been created? How often do they meet? Who makes final decisions?

5. What processes or professional development have addressed social justice of any kind—related to race, class, gender, sexual orientation, or disability? How successful have those been? How would you assess the readiness of your school community to address issues of social justice, particularly in the area of race and equity?

FURTHER READING

Ball, Stephen J. 1987. *The Micropolitics of Schools.* New York: Routledge.

Barth, Roland S. 1990. *Improving Schools from Within: Teachers, Parents, and Principals Can Make a Difference.* San Francisco: Jossey-Bass.

Bellah, Robert N., Richard Madsen, William M. Sullivan, Ann Swidler, and Steven M. Tipton. 1983. *Habits of the Heart: Individualism and Commitment in American Life.* New York: Harper and Row.

Brill, Fred. 2009. *Leading and Learning: Effective School Leadership Through Reflective Inquiry.* Portland, ME: Stenhouse.

Christensen, Linda. 1998. In Enid Lee, Deborah Menkart, and Margo Okazawa-Rey, eds., *Beyond Heroes and Holidays: A Practical Guide to K–12, Anti-Racist, Multicultural Education and Staff Development.* Washington, DC: Network of Educators on the Americas.

Dewey, John. 1938. *Experience and Education.* New York: Touchstone.

Ingersoll, Richard. 2003. *Who Controls Teachers' Work? Power and Accountability in America's Schools.* Cambridge, MA: Harvard University Press.

Little, Judith Warren. 2006. *Professional Development and Professional Development in a Learning-Centered School.* Washington, DC: National Education Association.

Spillane, James, and John B. Diamond. 2007. *Distributed Leadership in Practice.* New York: Teachers College Press.

TOOL 2-A: CRITICAL FRIENDS GROUP (CFG) PROTOCOLS: CONSULTANCY AND TUNING

All Critical Friends tools can be accessed at www.nsrfharmony.org (National School Reform Faculty) and http://www.nwrel.org/index.php (Northwest Regional Educational Laboratory).

A consultancy is a Critical Friends Group (CFG) process in which the presenter brings an *issue* for discussion. A tuning process is used the same way, except that it is used to give feedback on something written or visual—a plan, videotaped lesson, or student work. There should be time in the process for participants to read or view.

Because people new to the CFG processes must assume the role of facilitators, this script offers a way to start the process. Although it may seem awkward at first, it is a reminder of how the process moves forward. In later CFGs, it is a reminder. The presenter gives the facts of the issue and poses a problem for discussion. This is the script of the facilitator, who can use the exact words in the quoted portions below.

The attached process cards may be helpful to novice CFG groups.

Facilitator: "[Name] will present an issue for the discussants and to some degree for me to talk about. I will set time limits for each part of the process, keep time, decide if we can take a little more time on one parent, ask people to keep on task, and offer input. I may also redirect your questions and keep us in check as far as staying on the issue. I will ask the timekeeper to keep time and remind me." (*Facilitator reads steps.*)

PRESENTATION: Facilitator: "[Name] will present an issue for consultation (or plan, lesson, or tape for tuning). S/he will ask us to address a specific problem. After the presentation, which will last five minutes, we will have time for clarifying questions."

CLARIFYING QUESTION: Facilitator: "Now the discussants can ask clarifying or factual questions about the issue. This is not a time to give advice. You can ask, for example, have you tried _____? But it should not be framed as long advice about _____. If I feel you are straying into the feedback step, I will ask you to hold that for later."

FEEDBACK: Facilitator: "The presenter should now sit back from the group and listen and take notes. There might be a tendency to want to jump in, but the presenter should not do that. There will also be a tendency to need more information. I will make a judgment about the need for clarification and ask for more information and then get us back on track with feedback. The issue for consultancy is

Step	Content	Person	Time (can be adjusted)
I	Overview Reviews process; Presents sequence and any special circumstances.	Facilitator	2 minutes
2	Presentation of issue for consultancy: Presents facts and problem. Presentation of written or visual for tuning: Provides overview. Asks for specific assistance.	Presenter	5 minutes
3	Clarifying Questions These are factual questions about the situation.	Discussants ask presenter	5 minutes
4	Feedback/Discussion Offers warm and cool feedback. Presenter takes notes but does not join discussion.	Discussants	15 minutes
5	Presenter Reflection Says what is helpful. Discussants listen.	Presenter	5 minutes
6	Debriefing about the process. (This is the place that participants can adjust as long as they do not change the following: timed participation, presenter listening in step 4, and time for debriefing.)	All	5 minutes

_____, and _____ wants us to address this question: _____. Use warm and cool feedback; warm means good directions or ideas and cool means other or different ideas. If the discussion requires it, I may add two to three minutes, but then we will stop."

PRESENTER REFLECTION: Facilitator: "During this portion, the presenter will talk about what was helpful, what was appreciated, and what might be used. S/he may refer directly to participants or in general. It will be hard for the discussants not to jump in with more ideas. If the presenter finishes earlier than in five minutes, we will move to the debriefing process."

DEBRIEFING: Facilitator: "Now we will debrief on the process: what worked, what happened, and what each of us might have been feeling. We also may want to talk about what we can do in the next CFG without violating the basic tenets of the protocol: time-bound, rotation of discussion, and need for debriefing."

ROLES:

(1) The presenter presents issues and asks for specific feedback on the issue, responds to clarifying questions, stays quiet and takes notes while discussants give ideas, and responds to ideas and says what is helpful at the end.

(2) The timekeeper pays attention to times set for parts of protocol and asks the group if it wants to add one minute when it seems needed in any part of the protocol.

(3) The process checker makes certain that clarifying questions are not disguised as advice—that factual information about the issue is being requested. S/he may need to remind participants to give both warm and cool feedback and to remind the presenter to listen and take notes during discussion time and that discussants talk to each other, not to the presenter.

TOOL 2-B: EQUITY PRINCIPLES FOR TEACHERS

A school can use this tool as a needs assessment for its work on race and equity and a way to make careful decisions about focus. Or the staff can use the items on this survey to construct a survey useful to their school community.

Create a survey for the staff as an anonymous self-assessment on each item or the items that are appropriate for the readiness level of the staff with whom you work, using a five-point scale. The process for use involves:

- Bringing the aggregated anonymous data to a faculty meeting.
- Making generalizations about the data.
- Brainstorming priority areas for faculty direction by giving three small colored circles to everyone and having each participant put his or her three circles in areas that each considers a priority. Participants may use the circles in three different areas or put all in one area.
- Discussing priority areas and possible ways to address or take action. (Bring back to leadership team for discussion and further action.)
- Debriefing about how this process represents democracy and brings about consensus.

The following equity competencies for teachers, teacher-leaders, and principals refer to all forms of diversity: racial, cultural, language, ethnic, ableness, gender, and sexual preference.

Teachers, Teacher-Leaders, and Principals in Our School

- Have a clear sense of personal identity and seek ways to more completely understand that identity in the context of this school and society.

  ☐Never   ☐Sometimes   ☐Moderately   ☐Often   ☐Almost Always

- Regularly communicate high expectations for the success of ALL students and do not engage in blaming students or parents.

  ☐Never   ☐Sometimes   ☐Moderately   ☐Often   ☐Almost Always

- Are personally committed to achieving for all students and believe that school personnel are capable of making a difference in students' lives.

  ☐Never   ☐Sometimes   ☐Moderately   ☐Often   ☐Almost Always

- Develop personal bonds with students, understand and appreciate differences, and cease to view students as separate or other.

  ☐Never   ☐Sometimes   ☐Moderately   ☐Often   ☐Almost Always

- Are able and willing to construct curriculum and develop instructional practices that include the contributions and the perspectives of different cultural traditions that make up the society.

  ☐Never   ☐Sometimes   ☐Moderately   ☐Often   ☐Almost Always

- Explicitly teach students the culture of the school and make certain that students have experiences and content that assist them in understanding the dynamics of racism and prejudices as well as the dynamics of privilege and economic oppression.

  ☐Never   ☐Sometimes   ☐Moderately   ☐Often   ☐Almost Always

- Link academically challenging and antiracist curricula to the cultural, academic, and emotional assets that students bring to school, attending to higher-level cognitive development.

  ☐Never   ☐Sometimes   ☐Moderately   ☐Often   ☐Almost Always

- Involve parents and community in the students' education and give significant voice to those who are the caregivers of the students.

  ☐Never   ☐Sometimes   ☐Moderately   ☐Often   ☐Almost Always

- Are involved in social justice struggles outside of the classroom aimed at achieving an equitable and humane society.

  ☐Never   ☐Sometimes   ☐Moderately   ☐Often   ☐Almost Always

Adapted by Lynda Tredway, Principal Leadership Institute, UC Berkeley, from Zeichner, Gomez, and Melnick (1996).

TOOL 2-C: APPRECIATIVE/CONSTRUCTIVIST LISTENING

We know ourselves as social selves
Parents and children
Members of a people
Inheritors of a history and a culture
That we must nurture
Through memory and hope.

This uses the appreciative listening protocol with a personal narrative.

Read the above quote (from Bellah et al. 1985) aloud and have it on paper for all to read. Using appreciative or constructivist listening, talk for two minutes each using this prompt: *What history and culture that you have inherited do you want to nurture through memory and hope for your family, friends, or students?*

Norms for Engagement

1. Listen, fully, to a partner, sitting knee-to-knee, facing each other.

2. If there is silence in the designated time, that is fine. The listener may use nonverbal responses.

3. As the listener, do not comment, give feedback, or add your story; you are listening, not editing, giving your fullest personal attention to the speaker.

4. Maintain double confidentiality—you will not repeat a story you heard, and you will not ask your partner about the story he or she tells outside of this exercise unless he or she raises it again with you.

Facilitator Role

You will want to model this with a willing person if this is the first time you are doing appreciative or constructivist listening in this group.

Introduce this as a way to have someone listen to you completely without judgment for two minutes.

- Use a timer if at all possible.
- Ask participants to respond to the prompt.
- Then state norms for engagement. Ask if there are questions.
- Let everyone get settled face-to-face with a partner. If they do not know each other (or know each other well), give time for interchange to meet and greet before starting, and have the dyad decide who will go first. Be a "warm demander" on the use of duets/dyads.
- Join a single person if there is an uneven number.
- Do clear "bordering" of this activity by setting time or saying "Go" and then after two minutes saying "Stop" and changing partners.
- Debrief activity as a group. NOTE: There is often discomfort. Accept all responses; do not defend.

The website contains many facilitation protocols and suggestions that can help teachers entering this realm of leadership: http://www .managementhelp.org/grp_skll/facltate/facltate.htm#anchor106921.

TOOL 2-D: A COURAGE JOURNEY LINE

Something changes in me when I witness someone's courage.
                                                    —*Holly Near*

When I dare to be powerful to use my strength in the service of my vision, then it becomes less and less important whether I am afraid.

                                                    —*Audre Lorde*

Journey lines are used for a variety of our life experiences. You can do a journey line for reading, for leadership, or for anything you are trying to chart as a continuum. A journey to this point on any topic implies that the subject was a part of one's life early on.

Before deciding to do this exercise, complete the courage line yourself so that you work through an example before you tell others how to do it (see Figure 2.1). If available, play the Holly Near song "Change of Heart."

Give an example of a time in your life that you were courageous and took a risk. It can be about anything when you stood up for something you believed in.

Next, read these directions: "You are completing a journey line of courage. We know that courage in our lives came from a composite of experiences when we did take a stand or wished we had taken a stand. Learning from those experiences and charting them for ourselves as well as listening to the courage lines of others helps us beckon the daily courage to do our work together. The horizontal line describes age, and you should try to remember when you had an experience summoning courage. The vertical line becomes a graph of medium to high importance in developing your sense of yourself as a courageous person. The most important part of this is to think about four or five experiences in your life that demonstrated your personal courage. Again, they might be experiences when you wished you had been more courageous, or they might be experiences when you stood up for something. Of course, courage involves taking some kind of risk. Please take about eight min-utes to complete your personal journey line. After you have finished, choose one event to share with a pair or trio." (You may also choose to use the constructivist/appreciative listening protocol to share in duets/dyads.)

Norms for Engagement (Sharing)

1. We will maintain double confidentiality. You will share your journey line, but the person(s) you share with will not repeat your story to anyone else, and you will not ask the person(s) about it later unless he or she brings it up.

2. Assume the best intentions.

3. Give each contributor full attention and do not interrupt with your story.

Feel free to reinterpret the journey lines for other important aspects of your school or learning community.

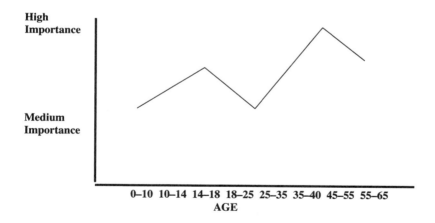

Figure 2.1. A Sample Journey Line

CHAPTER THREE

THINKING ABOUT SCHOOL RESOURCES

Money and Effectiveness

UNDER "NORMAL" CONDITIONS—in traditional and entrepreneurial schools—teachers don't have any reason to worry about how money is spent or what resources a school has. The district makes most of the resource decisions and allocates teachers and counselors, books, and computers to schools more or less on a per pupil basis, with perhaps a small discretionary fund that principals can spend for materials and field trips. Teachers participate in decisions only to the extent that the principal allows it; even schools with site councils are often rubber stamps for principals' decisions. In many entrepreneurial schools, educational management organizations or charter management organizations play the same role as districts do, allocating resources to schools. Under these conditions, there are no reasons for teachers to worry about money, resources, what's effective or what isn't, and the other topics of this chapter.

But in collective and collaborative schools (and in some entrepreneurial schools run on democratic principles), teachers have more say in the direction of the school, including resources and budget decisions. This is particularly true where districts have adopted school-based budgeting, allocating a substantial portion of the district's revenues to schools, which then have the authority to make decisions about how to spend them. Under these conditions schools can make decisions about trade-offs—whether, for example, to hire more teachers and fewer aides or to offer smaller classes only in the early grades rather than middling-sized classes in all grades, or whether to hire experienced but expensive teachers over inexperienced but cheaper teachers. Where principals take distributed leadership seriously, some of the leadership for budgeting is in the hands of teacher-leaders (for example, through membership on school-site councils). Then teachers as well as principals need to be able to think about the multiple resources in a school and the effective ways to use all resources, including money, to meet their school goals and needs.

Teachers have crucial roles to play in resource decisions for other reasons. It turns out, as the next section clarifies, that many of the most effective resources in schools are either *complex*, often related to instruction, or *abstract*, like school climate and trust. Complex and abstract resources cannot usually be bought in the way that smaller class size can be bought just by hiring more teachers. Instead, most complex and abstract resources need to be *constructed* by teachers and leaders working together. These are *collective* resources rather than improvements that can be made within individual classrooms. For example, the negative effects of tracking—a compound resource in our vocabulary, affecting students through lower teacher expectations, a (usually) watered-down curriculum, and peers with lower aspirations for postsecondary education—cannot be corrected by individual teachers but must rely on school decisions to replace current tracking practices with something else. School climate must be developed collectively because it involves norms and values that everyone in a school must share. Instructional improvements can be made by individual teachers, but they are much more powerful and consistent when all teachers in a school embrace them. Because many effective resources are collective and institutional rather than individual, all teachers need to understand what resources are effective, what their relationship to spending is, and what teachers can do to enhance these resources.

Once we understand that teachers in collective schools are involved in resource decisions, a deep paradox emerges. Most teachers, if they give it some thought, can identify many sources of waste in their schools. (See Tool 3-A, which readers should complete based on their own schools.) At the same time, many student needs are not being met—perhaps including more experienced or better-prepared teachers or ones less likely to leave; better physical facilities, labs, and equipment; professional development for teachers; or more support services for some students. How can there be both substantial waste and substantial unmet needs at the same time?

The question also emerges in the history of school spending. Real (inflation-adjusted) spending per pupil has almost quadrupled since 1959–1960, doubled since 1979–1980, and increased by almost one-third since 1989–1990, so no one can complain that spending has not gone up. But many teachers are still underpaid; inequalities in spending and in resources persist among schools, among districts, and among states; the conditions in most urban schools remain dire; and more money is necessary for reforms, ranging from updated computer and science labs to after-school and summer programs to health and mental health supports for students. Evidently, spending more money has not changed the nature of educational problems, the complaints about schools, or the patterns of inequity—and we are unlikely to be able to spend our way out of education problems in the future.

THE MONEY MYTH

**Key concept
Money Myth**

What's going on here? Our conceptions of money in education have been dominated by what we call the **Money Myth**: more funding is always better than less, inadequate outcomes can be explained by inadequate revenues, and the solution to any educational problem requires increasing spending (Grubb 2009). The Money Myth arose during the nineteenth and early twentieth centuries, when public schools were expanding rapidly. Raising enough money to provide simple access to all who wanted to attend was a serious challenge. This continued to be a problem with the expansion of the high school after 1900, especially during the 1930s, when public revenues were scarce. But. except in a few fast-growing areas of the country, the problem is no longer finding enough seats for everyone. Rather, the problems facing schools are those of *quality*—of increasing the rigor of schools, or teaching new skills (the "skills of the twenty-first century")—and of *equity*, particularly narrowing achievement gaps among students. So the challenge has shifted from one of ensuring access to one of ensuring higher quality and better outcomes for all, but our thinking about money and resources has not continued to develop.

In this chapter, then, we first examine the nature of resources—those aspects of schools that affect student outcomes as distinct from money—in order to develop a more complex view of what happens within schools. In the second section we examine which resources might be effective in enhancing students' outcomes; some resources (even those that are widely supported, like class size reduction or teacher aides) may in fact not be effective. We then turn to evidence about what money can buy and what it cannot, and examine the issues of racial and ethnic differences in outcomes, arguing that practices related to racial and ethnic treatment should also be considered among the important resources in a school.

We conclude by summarizing the equity effects of resource issues.

SIMPLE, COMPOUND, COMPLEX, AND ABSTRACT RESOURCES

A great deal of concern about equity in education has focused on inequalities in spending per student, another
manifestation of the Money Myth. As early as 1905, Ellwood Cubberley, one of the first to understand that public funds are often unequally distributed, declared that
"the question of sufficient revenue lies back of almost
every other [educational] problem." During the 1930s,
school finance experts began focusing on state funding,
devising formulas for states to allocate revenues to districts so as to equalize the uneven spending patterns resulting from differences in local property tax bases. In
the late 1960s a different tactic emerged: litigation as a
way to force state legislators to equalize funding. Litigation often arises in education when legislative approaches
fail to generate equitable results—equitable access to facilities (as in desegregation cases), or equitable allocations
of revenue, or (rarely) the equitable allocation of real resources like qualified teachers, textbooks and materials,
and adequate physical facilities in *Williams v. California*.
The first blockbuster case about spending inequalities
arose in California with *Serrano v. Priest*, in which the
California Supreme Court declared in 1973 that the
state's funding of schools was unconstitutional because
the differences among districts in property tax bases
made the quality of education a function of where different students lived. The *Serrano* strategy was repeated in
many other states, though often lawyers had to return to
court repeatedly to enforce earlier decisions—up to
eleven times in New Jersey, four times in New Hamp-
shire, three times in Texas, and at least twice in many
other states (Yinger 2004, 387–389).

Other litigation strategies have emerged in recent years, especially so-called adequacy approaches arguing that state constitutions—for example, the language in some states requiring a "thorough and efficient education"—require states to ensure an adequate education for all students (Minorini and Sugarman 1999). Of course, defining "adequate" levels of education has itself been contentious and ambiguous. Over time our conception of adequate education has shifted considerably—from providing the 3 R's in the eighteenth century to a wider variety of curricula, from including only a subset of children to accommodating the special needs of students with disabilities and those speaking foreign languages, from providing log cabins and outdoor privies to constructing sleek buildings with science and computer labs and sports facilities. Adequacy has been a moving target, and these lawsuits have to wrestle with the question of how to define adequacy.

What is remarkable is how little equalization all this litigation has created. In some states litigation has indeed prompted legislatures to equalize funding. In a few cases—Kentucky and New Jersey are probably the best examples—legislatures have responded by instituting many other reforms. In other states legislative responses have been slow and grudging, and there hasn't been much equalization. Even in states where funding has become more equal, it's difficult to detect any real equalization in the resources that money can buy. In five states where lawsuits caused inequality in *spending* per pupil to decrease, inequalities in *outcomes*—test scores and dropout rates—have remained the same (Yinger 2004; Grubb 2009, ch. 11). Even though litigation appears to be a strong way to assert equity claims and to equalize funding and then outcomes, it has accomplished remarkably little.

One reason for these noneffects is the limited impact of litigation on legislative responses—an issue for lawyers and political experts to confront. But a second reason is the heart of this chapter: the conversion of more equal *spending* into those school *resources* that affect student outcomes has been uncertain. *Money, after all, does not itself educate students. The resources that money might buy—teachers with specific characteristics, particular curricula, science labs and computer labs, and revised occupational workshops—can educate students, though we will clarify that some resources educate students even though money cannot buy them outright.* And though courts may have some jurisdiction over money, with only a few exceptions (like the *Williams* case in California) they have been able to specify how money might be translated into effective school resources. In reality, then, the distance from litigation with egalitarian intentions to court decisions with egalitarian requirements, to state legislative action that meets these requirements, and to the conversion of equalized *revenues* into effective school *resources* is long and complex—and the effectiveness of litigation can break down at any one of these points.

Focus point

Litigation thus is not generally a solution to inequalities in schooling outcomes. For many of the same reasons, efforts by states and the federal government to spend their way to more successful schools often have been ineffective. In California, for example, there has been a series of multibillion-dollar efforts to improve schools, including class size reduction and reforms focusing on the lowest-performing school; whereas some schools have been able to take advantage of these funds, the effects on average have been zero. Similarly, the efforts by the federal government over more than four decades to improve the education of "disadvantaged" students through its Chapter 1 program have had very few clear effects, and there's no evidence that No Child Left Behind has improved test scores or narrowed the achievement gap (Grubb 2009, ch. 10). Therefore, because the old ways—the patterns established by the Money Myth—are ineffective, we need to develop new ways of thinking about money and resources.

One way to start is to examine the table in Tool 3-B. Some years ago Eric Hanushek (1989) summarized a vast amount of research about the effects of various resources on student outcomes. (The underlying research is statistical, and we will not review the technical details here except to note one serious flaw: all these results are based on standardized test scores as the measure of student outcomes. To see how results change with a much greater variety of outcome measures, see Grubb 2009, 70–72.) But how can it be that of 65 studies that examined the effects of spending per student on test scores, only 13 found spending to be positively related to outcomes? Three even found that higher spending *reduced* test scores! This finding challenges the Money Myth directly, as well as every educator's "common sense" understanding that more money could be spent for more academic coaches, more professional development, and better materials that would surely enhance learning. The puzzle hardly ends there. Smaller class sizes—beloved by teachers for obvious reasons, and a favorite approach of many policymakers— proved effective in only 14 of 152 studies; in 13 cases, fewer students per teacher led to *worse* outcomes. Similarly for the other simple resources in the table: it's hard to find much support for spending additional money on teacher education, administrative inputs, or facilities. Only teacher experience, where 40 of 140 studies confirmed a positive effect on test scores, might be worth spending money on, according to these results.

Every educator should wrestle with the puzzles presented by this table and come to his or her own conclusions about what might explain these counterintuitive results. Careful consideration suggests why so many studies have found simple school resources to be ineffective. If instructors continue to teach the same way (for example, through lecture with routine questioning) in smaller classes, then class size reduction may have no effect. If some experienced teachers become skilled while others are burned out—a common problem facing principals with a veteran teacher workforce—then, without ascertaining the practices among experienced teachers,

experience may have no effect, on average. If teacher education is concerned with content knowledge but fails to
improve pedagogical practices, then it might not influence instruction. So class size, experience, and teacher
preparation may not influence teacher practices in the
ways we (naively) think they might. Furthermore, it is
necessary to go into the classroom in some way to see
whether experienced teachers are better at using a variety
of instructional approaches or are burned out, to see
whether teachers teach differently in small classes, and to
learn whether teachers with more professional development or higher degrees change their teaching practices.
Educators at the school level might be able to learn about
such practices through classroom observation, but conventional researchers, who do not use classroom observation or who cannot otherwise learn what happens within
classrooms, cannot.

There turn out to be multiple reasons for the counterintuitive result that increased spending does not lead directly to better outcomes. The first, as responding to the
first question in Tool 3-A should clarify, is that there are
many forms of waste in public schools. Sometimes
money is spent on ineffective resources, such as incompetent teachers, weak after-school programs, or teacher
aides, without clear plans. Money may be spent without
changing practices, for example, when outdated forms of
professional development—bringing in outside experts
for one-shot, one-hour afternoon workshops—are used
for complex changes like improving instruction. Often,
money is spent piecemeal, when schools respond to categorical grants by buying whatever the funding dictates
without an overall plan, or districts provide year-end
money that must be quickly (and wastefully) spent. District and school audits of waste would surely uncover a
great deal of spending that could be redirected to other
uses.

A large category of waste involves another abstract resource: *stability*. Resources may be spent on changes with

potential long-run benefits, like improving school climate or changing instruction. But with instability—a new principal taking a different direction, a superintendent with different priorities and strategic plans (discussed in Chapter 5), or teacher turnover—those resources are effectively wasted. Urban schools are particularly plagued with instability as students move around due to housing problems; teachers leave for better "working conditions" (often a euphemism for more middle-class and white students); principals leave; superintendents and board members come and go; and policies, programs, and professional development change with them or need to be repeated for new personnel.

Second, schools often spend more money on expensive but ineffective programs—even counterproductive programs. Traditional vocational education has provided a clear example, spending more on equipment and materials while reducing student learning and progress through high school. Other forms of tracking have similar effects: the general track with its watered-down curriculum, remedial pedagogy with its emphasis on drill and practice for students who have previously failed to learn through this method, and many interventions spending more money for students who are behind but without producing improved results.

Third, sometimes the problem is that schools need *compound* resources rather than the *simple* resources in Hanushek's table. Class size reduction provides a good case study of how resources work. In a multibillion-dollar "experiment" in California, class size reduction failed to improve outcomes on the average because many districts hired inexperienced teachers, lacked professional development to help teachers teach differently in small classes, and stuffed the new classes into inappropriate spaces like closets and auditoriums (Stecher and Bohrnstedt 2002). The effective resource is not simple class size reduction but a *compound* resource: smaller classes *plus* well-educated teachers *plus* professional development focused on teaching in small classes *plus* adequate facilities. Similarly, an **effective resource** is teacher education *focused on instructional practices*, or what teachers sometimes call pedagogical content knowledge (Little 2006), not just any form of professional development. Another resource is experience *used to enhance a repertoire of teaching approaches*, not experience by itself. Computers (not included in Hanushek's survey) provide a final obvious example: providing computers without professional development for teachers and without technical support to keep the computers operating is pointless; the potentially effective *compound* resource requires more than simply installing computers.

Key concept
effective resource

Fourth, most districts and schools fail to realize the power of **complex resources**. Complex resources are those that are difficult to change because they are deeply embedded in beliefs and institutional practices. Among the most important complex resources are those related to instruction, which are notoriously difficult to change. Teacher use of time, teacher control over instruction, departmental encouragement of innovation, and teachers' use of innovative (or "balanced") instruction all lead to improved learning and higher test scores (Grubb 2009, ch. 2). But these complex resources cannot be readily bought, and districts with higher spending per student do not automatically have higher levels of these resources. Instead, they must be constructed at the school level, by principals and teachers working collaboratively over time, using the right approaches to staff development, and providing feedback to one another (particularly through classroom observations) about improvements in instruction.

Key concept
complex resources

Fifth, **abstract resources** are powerful, too—abstract in the sense that they describe conditions in schools that can be described and measured but refer to concepts rather than resources that can be touched or seen. Examples include positive school climate, an absence of negative distractions like fighting and drug-dealing, an unfair discipline system (see Chapter 6), overall student

Key concept
abstract resources

commitment to schooling, trust among a school's participants, the coherence of the curriculum, and (again) stability among students, teachers, leaders, and reforms. Like
complex resources, abstract resources cannot be bought,
and higher spending does not increase them. They are
largely embedded in the personal relationships of the
adults and the students in the schools and therefore must
be constructed through careful school-level diagnosis of
what is going wrong, development of appropriate
changes, and then collaboration among teachers and leaders. Some money may be necessary—sometimes releasing
teachers for joint planning, occasionally for materials,
sometimes bringing in outside experts—but spending
will make no difference without diagnosis, agreement,
leadership, and collective action. There's no market in
which to buy a positive school climate, and no substitute
for teachers and leaders working collaboratively.

Thus, many factors explain why the relationship between money and student outcomes is so weak, and many
resources that are effective in enhancing outcomes—only
some of which (simple and compound resource) can be
readily bought. This conclusion provides teacher-leaders a
powerful role to play in making schools more effective
and more equitable. *Teachers and school-level leaders are in
better positions than are researchers, or district officials, or
state and federal administrators, to understand what happens within classrooms and schools, to understand what resources they have and what they lack.* Tool 3-C provides a
framework for developing a comprehensive *resource audit*
of a school, very different from a *fiscal audit* examining
revenues and expenditures only. With such an audit,
teachers and leaders are in better positions to construct
the complex and abstract resources necessary for effective
schools and to identify which simple resources are ineffective because a compound resource is necessary instead.
Part of being an active teacher, or a *professional* teacher
able to enhance the effectiveness of schools, is recognizing

Focus point

the many resources that contribute to students' progress, and then acting to enhance these resources.

EFFECTIVENESS, EVIDENCE, AND IMPLEMENTATION

One central problem in developing both effective and equitable schools is to put *effective* resources in place rather than wasteful or counterproductive uses of money. But this apparently simple requirement presents at least three distinct problems: first, understanding what school practices and programs are effective; then, putting these resources in place; and, finally, determining whether they are equitably distributed. Each part of this requirement has its own difficulty, and teachers who take on the role of teacher-leaders—and certainly those who are or aspire to be principals—need to be clear about these.

First of all, the evidence about what is effective is itself contentious. At one extreme, some researchers believe that no evidence can be counted unless it has been generated by random assignment methods, in which students are assigned either to an "experimental" group that receives a particular "treatment" (like a specific after-school program, or classrooms of different sizes) or to a "control" group with no special treatment. Sometimes such studies provide some guidance (see, for example, Quint 2006, summarizing studies of national reform efforts), but in many cases no random assignment studies are available. Quite apart from the ethical issues in running random assignment experiments and the Dr. Frankenstein aspects of having "experimental" groups, other researchers think that limiting evidence to random assignment experiments is too narrow and that it neglects a great deal of potentially useful information, including all qualitative results.

Another approach to evidence relies on statistical analysis. The data in Tool 3-B come from many statistical analyses, but they have similar flaws: they all rely on standardized test scores as measures of outcomes, and virtually all examine only a restricted set of simple resources. The results about simple, compound, complex, and abstract resources in this chapter also come from statistical analysis (Grubb 2009) but are based on a much richer data set with many student outcomes and a much larger set of school resources.

Sometimes there is useful information from surveys of the literature, even if there are no clear conclusions about effectiveness. For example, an enormous literature on out-of-school-time (OST) programs, including after-school programs that many schools use to close the achievement gap, has found very little evidence of powerful programs. But it has still generated useful conclusions about what contributes to effectiveness: a clear mission, high academic expectations, positive social norms, a safe and healthy environment, a small total enrollment, stable and well-prepared personnel, appropriate content and pedagogy related to the program's goals, integrated family and community involvement, and frequent assessment (e.g., Bodilly and Beckett 2005). The reviews of particular literatures, like those published in the *Review of Educational Research* and the new *Journal of Research on Educational Effectiveness*, are often the quickest ways to see what the preponderance of the research has said about effectiveness. Sometimes educators use evidence about the general characteristics of effective programs to make recommendations about specific programs that fit the same profile; for example, the National Research Council (2004) summary of motivation and engagement in high schools can be used to judge whether certain approaches (like theme-based approaches) are more motivating than others (like "remedial" pedagogies based on drill and practice). These forms of evidence are not "proof" based on statistical methods, but they do provide careful reasoning from accumulated experience about what is likely to work.

Sometimes schools generate their own evidence, which can be more timely and tailored to the unique context of a school than academic research. This includes teacher action research, whereby teachers investigate the effects of their own practices and those of their colleagues on their students, using methods that are less formal than those of university-based researchers but that still try to consider alternative explanations and different solutions. A similar method exists for aspiring principals; for example, in leadership action research projects in the Principal Leadership Institute, aspiring leaders take problems in their schools, devise solutions corresponding to what they know about causes, implement the solutions over four to five months, and collect evidence of the effects. Some districts conduct research, and this too may be close to the experiences of schools. The federal government, with its economies of scale, also conducts and funds a great deal of research about "what works," including a What Works Clearinghouse—though its efforts under the Bush administration were marred by ideological positions and a rigid preference for random assignment methods.

However, other forms of "evidence" that educators use are considerably less rigorous. Some organizations, for example, have looked at test scores as the only measure of outcomes and have held up a few high-scoring schools as examples of what other schools should do, without careful evidence of the causal connection between test scores and school specifics and without considering year-to-year variation in school test scores. The literature on "high-flying schools" and "90-90-90" schools—90 percent free- and reduced-lunch students, 90 percent racial minorities, and 90 percent of students meeting state standards—suffers from this problem, because data for several years in a row reveal that there are very few such schools. Even though the findings may seem appropriate—particularly the conclusion that successful elements in 90-90-90 schools "come down to teaching and leadership variables that cannot be sold by vendors nor purchased by schools," a conclusion remarkably similar to ours—the underlying evidence is still weak (Jerald 2001; Harris 2006; Reeves 2004; Reeves 2009). Another tendency, useful for ideas but not for decision-making, is to take the advice of friends in neighboring schools, or nearby districts, without asking (as teacher-research or action research projects would) about the nature of evidence. Yet another is to believe the producers of programs and textbooks, again without asking whether their proclamations ("Proven Practices!!") have any basis in evidence. Sometimes educators may take the word of an agency that has presumably sifted through the evidence, such as a state agency or the federal What Works Clearinghouse, even though conclusions have been politically influenced.

The problem of evidence for effective practices is not, then, a simple question. Nor is there an easy source of evidence, because the federal clearinghouse is seriously flawed, states and districts have not yet developed similar clearinghouses, and research results are often poorly written and difficult to find. Nonetheless, teachers and principals trying to make their schools more effective and trying to allocate scarce resources (including but not limited to money) to enhance effective practices always need to be aware of the strengths and limitations of their evidence. Otherwise, they may end up unwittingly contributing to the waste that plagues so many American schools.

Determining which resources are effective is only the first step. The second challenge is to put these resources in place. For some resources, this is not a special problem because most *simple* resources can be readily bought. For example, a lower pupil/adult ratio proves to enhance the progress of students, presumably by personalizing the school, and more teachers and counselors can be readily hired. Paying higher salaries, as a way to expand the pool of applicants for teaching positions and reducing turnover (and increasing experience), also proves to be effective, and increasing the salary schedule is an easy (if expensive) thing to do. Teacher planning time and student use of counseling are two other effective resources that cost additional money in obvious ways. In sum, when an activity is known to enhance student outcomes *and* that activity requires specific expenditures, then increased spending is effective. Similarly, in the case of compound resources, each element can be independently bought: more teachers to reduce class size, more intensive recruitment efforts to maintain the quality of teachers, professional development to enable teachers to teach more effectively in smaller classes, and provision of adequate space. As long as schools and districts remember that some effective resources are *compound* and require several elements, these resources can still be purchased.

Complex and abstract resources are quite different. For instructional improvement, having teachers control their own instruction requires decisions by districts and principals and appropriate professional development as well as teacher collaboration; it cannot be "bought" the way smaller classes can be. Moving away from traditional teaching methods usually requires appropriate professional development, practice, observation, and feedback from peers or from master teachers, and steady development over time. It's not something that can be accomplished quickly, and it's probably less effective if individual teachers attempt to do this than if they do it as part of a schoolwide effort. A similar situation affects abstract resources, such as school climate, negative distractions like fights and drug-dealing, overall student commitment to schooling, trust among members of a school community, and the coherence of the curriculum. These resources refer to abstract characteristics of schools rather than teachers who can be seen or materials that can be hefted. They are largely embedded in the personal relationships among members of a school community. But again, they are impossible to purchase; instead they require leadership, vision, and collaboration within a school. Such efforts may have to be repeated each year because of turnover of staff and students. Because complex and abstract resources cannot be bought, districts with higher levels of spending per pupil do not necessarily have higher levels of such resources—another case where money and effective resources are not related. Instead, complex resources must be constructed by teachers and school leaders—and sometimes district officials as well—acting collectively.

A third requirement for equitable schools is to ascertain whether *effective* resources are equitably distributed or not—this is the issue of distributive equity to which we return in Chapter 6. Of course, spending per student is inequitably distributed and has been the focus of many lawsuits challenging spending differences. It turns out, however, that the worst inequalities are not those of money. Although there are some urban districts with very low levels of spending, on the average, urban districts have slightly *higher* expenditures per pupil than do suburban districts. In 2003–2004, for example, central city schools spent $7,812 per pupil, compared with $7,542 in suburban schools and $7,268 in all schools (Jacob 2007, table 1). At the same time, this higher level of spending did not lead to more real resources: central city schools had higher numbers of students per teacher (15.0 versus 14.6), lower teacher salaries ($45,400 versus $46,100, despite higher costs in cities), a higher proportion of schools with temporary buildings (37.7 percent versus 34.4 percent), and a higher proportion of schools using common spaces for instruction (21.3 percent versus 19 percent)—yet another illustration that money and resources are not necessarily correlated.

Similarly, in looking across a random sample of high school students, expenditure per student adjusted for cost differences among districts is (along with instructional expenditures per student) one of the most *equally* distributed resources, even though spending is considered by most observers to be highly unequal. There's also

Complex resources must be constructed by teachers and school leaders— and sometimes district officials as well—acting collectively.

relatively little variation in teacher salary levels, in teacher education levels, or in the extent of teacher certification (Grubb 2009, table 1.1). But as we shift from these simple resources to compound, complex, and abstract resources, levels of inequality among students go up. Teacher experience in secondary education—a compound resource resulting from experience plus staying in secondary teaching—is much more unequally distributed than is spending per student; professional development is also much more unequal. Among the complex resources related to instruction, teachers' use of time, encouragement of innovative teaching, overall teacher innovation, and innovative math teaching are still more unequally distributed. Some abstract resources—the presence of negative events like fighting and drug-dealing, and school problems as reported by principals—are also highly unequally distributed. So, surprising though it may be, spending per pupil is among the most equally distributed resources, followed by other simple resources; compound resources and, in particular, the complex resources related to teaching are the most unequally distributed. Following the usual patterns in American schools, we might expect them to be unequally distributed among white, black, and Latino students.

There's corroboration for such findings in books like *Savage Inequalities*: what Jonathan Kozol (1991) and other authors portray in books illustrating the unacceptable conditions in urban schools is not just the effects of money but the conditions of overwhelmed teachers, incoherent instruction, disorderly school climates, a pervasive alienation from learning among students, and (often) incompetent administrations unable to change the conditions of these schools. The problem is not sufficient revenues; it is that these revenues are being spent for ineffective practices. One obvious target in trying to eliminate the multiple achievement gaps in American schools, then, is to identify and then remedy the large number of inequalities in school resources, extending well beyond money.

RACIAL AND ETHNIC DIMENSIONS
OF EFFECTIVE RESOURCES

It's no secret that the most profound inequalities in the American educational system—those illustrated in Tool 1-B—are associated with racial and ethnic status. The "achievement gap" is usually stated in terms of differences among white, African American, and Latino students in test scores, or—to take a different dimension of the gap—in the differences between the high school dropout rates of white students and Latino students. The efforts under No Child Left Behind to bring all students up to proficiency by 2014 are largely aimed at the racial and ethnic gaps in American schooling. This is another reason why no effort to make schools more effective, or more equitable, can ignore the racial and ethnic dimensions of inequality.

When we try to understand these racial and ethnic gaps, some part of them can be explained by family background—particularly by differences in parental education and in parental aspirations for their children, which contribute in powerful ways to almost every aspect of school success. Parental occupation and income have smaller effects on schooling outcomes, as does coming from a female-headed family. Students who move from school to school do worse than stable students, as they have to adjust to new schools and start a new curriculum, so the housing instability that afflicts some low-income families is detrimental to schooling in obvious ways. Schools can't usually do much about these parental influences, although a few have tried to develop programs, like Puente in California, that enhance parental aspirations for their children in a structured support system. (Puente works by having more experienced immigrant parents convince new immigrants about the importance of schooling in the United States, for their daughters as well as their sons.) The importance of family background for schooling is one reason why we will return to the subject of nonschool policies in Chapter 6, when we summarize what social justice implies for a wide range of U.S. policies.

A second cause of racial and ethnic gaps includes all the differences in school resources that exist among schools, districts, and states. There's a substantial history of writing about the desolate conditions in urban schools compared with their suburban counterparts. Kozol wrote about these differences in the 1960s, in *Death at an Early Age* (1967), and then revisited this topic again in *Savage Inequalities* (1991). Many other journalists have taken up the same argument, writing about the intolerable conditions in their local schools. Over this same period a large number of lawsuits have been filed, usually against state governments, for allowing spending disparities in districts to be so large, and the evidence underlying these lawsuits has included stories of underprepared and overwhelmed teachers along with dilapidated facilities—including disgusting bathrooms, inadequate textbooks, and outdated lab equipment and vocational workshops.

But even after considering the effects of family background and unequal school resources, there are still racial and ethnic differences in test scores, in progress through school, and in the attitudes and aspirations that shape life after high school. Family background and school resources fail to explain between 45 percent and 60 percent of the black-white differences in test scores, 25 percent to 40 percent of white-Latino differences, 45 percent of the black-white difference in earning a high school diploma, and 20 percent of the white-Latino difference (Grubb 2009, table B-4). *An irreducible knot of racial and ethnic inequality remains after considering almost every possible alternative explanation. The persistence of such differences demands that everyone—every teacher, every principal, every researcher, every district and state administrator with responsibility for narrowing achievement gaps—come up with some explanation of what might explain this remaining gap.* Some commentators have, of course, tried to explain such differences as genetic, which has been a persistent

Focus point

explanation in the sorry history of American race relations. However, the empirical evidence against genetic
reasons is by now overwhelming, so other explanations
are necessary.

Focus point

*When we look at the qualitative evidence about what
happens in schools, as well as at our own experiences inside
schools, one powerful explanation involves the mistreatment
of students—based on class differences, sometimes, and certainly on gender differences, but most often based on race
and ethnicity.* There's substantial testimony about mistreatment from African American and Latino writers re-
membering their own schooling, from ethnographers
describing particular schools and districts, from critical
race theory with its insistence on personal stories and
voice, and from our own observations in schools and
community colleges. Mistreatment takes many forms, so
it can be elusive. Sometimes it may be overt and con-
scious, as in the physical abuse of students, but it's more
likely to take the form of covert and unconscious mistreatment, sometimes called "micro-aggressions"—
individually small but collectively relentless (Solorzano
2001). Many students of color report feeling invisible or
ignored in the classroom, with their concerns about race
marginalized. These students are more likely to feel demeaned for using vernacular English or home languages.
The sense that schools are trying to replace a student's
home culture with mainstream middle-class norms
(rather than encouraging multiple identities or multiculturalism) has been labeled "subtractive schooling," which
has been documented in the historically persistent "mismatch" between the culture of schooling and the culture
of some students' communities (Valenzuela 1999; Deschenes, Cuban, and Tyack 2001).

Racial minority students are less likely to find racially
similar adults who can serve as mentors, sponsors, pro-
tectors, and role models. Their teachers, who are pre-
dominantly white, are likely to have a range of cultural
and racial misconceptions. Students of color are more
likely to be the victims of the well-documented problem

of lower teacher expectations (Ferguson 2000; Weinstein 2002). They are more likely to be disciplined and to be suspended or expelled for infractions that other students are not punished for, particularly under "zero-tolerance" policies. These processes start early: in Ann Ferguson's ethnography *Bad Boys*, the school practices that set students up for failure became evident by fourth grade as boys were "adultified"—treated as if they were already adult criminals rather than rambunctious boys.

Many commentators have blamed teachers for these different forms of mistreatment. This is sometimes true, though we think that reality is more complex. Schools (and urban schools in particular) are often pressure cookers where teachers are under enormous stress. Sometimes teacher education programs prepare them to understand their African American and Latino students better, but very little prepares them to know how best to foster academic English or challenges to their authority. Many aspects of teaching are automatic and unconscious, and without assistance (particularly classroom observation and feedback) even the best teachers may unconsciously treat students in different ways that reinforce discrimination. We need to remember that race relations are among the most difficult issues in our country, and it's unfair to ask teachers to solve this problem when the rest of the citizenry has not.

Although it seems self-evident that the mistreatment of students would reduce their engagement with teachers and their commitment to schooling in general, the psychological conception of identity threat clarifies how this happens. In Claude Steele's (1997) influential analysis, individuals have many identities, some of them neutral in some settings (for example, a lover of music or art, an athlete) and some of them negative in other settings (like being African American or Latino in schools, or being an immigrant unable to speak English fluently in the workplace, or being a girl in math and science classes). *Stereotype threat* describes the tendency of individuals in a negatively stereotyped group to perform poorly or to withdraw from an activity if the negative stereotype is triggered by some action or word—for example, by the disparagement of teachers, or low performance on tests labeled as critical to future success. In a diverse society with so many stereotypes with positive and negative meanings, stereotype threat—including micro-aggressions, "subtractive schooling" as teachers socialize students to mainstream norms, and unconscious mistreatment—is almost inevitable *unless* something is done to prevent it.

That's the bad news. The good news is that different forms of mistreatment and stereotype threat help explain the racial/ethnic gaps in American schooling. Advocates have developed an enormous range of strategies to combat these forms of mistreatment head on and to avoid triggering stereotype threat. These include finding more teachers of color, to be sure, but also a variety of curricular and pedagogical innovations: explicit attention to code-switching for immigrant students and speakers of black vernacular English, to avoid punitive correction of non-standard English; an enormous range of culturally relevant pedagogy and multicultural education that brings new curriculum materials; new subjects (like the role of race in American society); pedagogies with greater student participation and more critical perspectives; systematic classroom observations so that teachers can learn if they are unconsciously mistreating students of color; different approaches to discipline, less demeaning and more respectful of norms in black and Latino communities; nonteaching support from same-race counselors and mentors; and—to get schools started on the difficult process of adopting such approaches—"courageous conversations" about racial dilemmas and the reasons for racial gaps (see Chapter 2 for an explanation of "courageous conversations").

Cross-Reference
For a parallel
discussion of the
challenges faced
by English
language
learners in
schools see
Book 2,
Chapter 1.

Focus point

These racially supportive practices constitute a vast portfolio of options for schools and districts that take the racial and ethnic dimensions of achievement gaps seriously. In the framework we have used in this chapter, these are complex and abstract resources of the most difficult kind, which again must be constructed by teachers and leaders working together within specific schools because these resources cannot be bought. Sometimes money is necessary—for outside experts, facilitators of difficult racial conversations, release time, or curriculum materials. These purchases will be wasted if the relationships among adults in the school are weak and mistrusting. The crucial resources in confronting racial and ethnic differences head on are not money, but other abstract resources: agreement within a school that racial issues must be confronted; clear diagnosis of where the problems come from; consideration of the varied practices that might address mistreatment; and vision, persistence, cooperation, and widespread trust.

THE IMPLICATIONS OF RESOURCES FOR EQUITY

It seems we have returned to Ellwood Cubberley's contention that "the question of sufficient revenue lies back of almost every other educational problem"—except that the question of sufficient *effective resources* is the crucial issue. Districts and schools that want to become more effective, and more effective for low-performing students—and the teachers, teacher-leaders, and principals who make these schools run—need to understand a broader array of resources beyond the simple resources that money can buy. The need in many cases for compound resources, composed of several related simple resources, implies that educators must constantly be thinking about whether particular resources are necessary but not sufficient; investing in only one component of a compound resource is likely to lead to waste. Recognizing a wide array of complex and abstract resources is crucial to understanding the effectiveness of schools. The agenda of creating more equitable schools is particularly dependent on recognizing a wide array of resources because compound, complex, and abstract resources are generally more inequitably distributed than are simple resources, including spending per student (the object of so much litigation).

Recognizing a wide array of complex and abstract resources is crucial to understanding the effectiveness of schools.

Furthermore, teachers and teacher-leaders play special roles in constructing some of the most important resources in schools. The complex resources related to instruction, especially moving toward innovative and "balanced" instruction, require teacher dedication and participation, even though principals as instructional leaders may be crucial too. The abstract resources of supportive school climate, student commitment, internal alignment and trust, curricula coherence, and stability cannot be constructed without the participation of teachers, or by teachers acting independently; they require widespread cooperation of teachers, plus the vision and leadership that principals and teacher-leaders can provide. Once again, new kinds of schools, more effective and more equitable than traditional schools, require new kinds of teachers and leaders to create them.

Finally, perhaps the most crucial elements of social justice in education—the racial and ethnic gaps in achievement and progress through schooling—have been among the most resistant to change. One problem is diagnosis, because the conventional explanations—variations in class dimensions associated with race and ethnicity and variations in school resources—cannot explain away racial and ethnic differences. Other explanations must be developed, and the one that seems most persuasive to us—because of the qualitative evidence and the evident alienation of many working-class black and Latino students from formal schooling—is the mistreatment of these students, in ways ranging from small but persistent ("microaggressions") to large and devastating, especially in disciplinary issues. But here too teachers and teacher-leaders can play crucial roles in reconstructing schools using the abstract resources of equitable and supportive treatment of racial minority students.

It has become common to say that teachers are the most important resources in public schooling. But what counts is not only the presence of teachers who can mind their own classrooms, motivate their own students, and teach in ways that respect and support all students. Just as important is the ability of teachers to move outside their classrooms, to participate with their colleagues and leaders in constructing effective resources at the school level. Once again, education is not just about people; it's about the way these people interact collectively inside institutions with particular practices.

DISCUSSION QUESTIONS

1. What process is now used to allocate both funding and other resources in your school? What roles do teachers play? How might these be changed to allow better information on effective resources to be used?

2. How much discretion does your district allow your school in how to spend *money*? In how to determine the *resources* in your schools?

3. If you were to develop an instructional improvement plan for your school, what two or three priorities would be at the top of your list? What evidence do you have that they are especially effective? What would you need—what money, what support from school or district leadership, what cooperation from teachers, what other outside resources—to put these priorities in place?

4. What do the data at your school show about the academic performance of students of color? About their progress through school—for example, rates of being held back or rates of accumulating credits in high school? About other dimensions of school performance, like disciplinary referrals? How would you explain the differences among groups of students in these outcome measures? What different practices and policies might address these causes?

FURTHER READING

Grubb, W. Norton. 2009. *The Money Myth: School Resources, Outcomes, and Equity.* New York: Russell Sage Foundation.

Kozol, Jonathan. 1991. *Savage Inequalities: Children in America's Schools.* New York: HarperPerennial.

Little, J. W. 2006. *Professional Development and Professional Community in the Learning-Centered School.* Washington, DC: National Education Association.

TOOL 3-A: IDENTIFYING SOURCES OF WASTE IN SCHOOLS

Identify several examples of waste at your school or district—that is, funds that are or have been misused, or used ineffectively, or used for activities, personnel, or programs that are ineffective.

What were the factors causing the waste? Which of these sources of waste were the result of *school-level* decisions and can be corrected by school decisions? Which of them are the responsibilities of the *district,* and require solutions outside of the school's control?

What kind of planning process or budgeting mechanism would enable your school or district to avoid the waste you identify?

What does all this say about the conclusion, sometimes based on Hanushek's review (see Tool 3-B), that school resources don't make much difference to educational outcomes?

TOOL 3-B: THE (IN)EFFECTIVENESS OF SIMPLE RESOURCES

Table 3.1 was developed by reviewing 187 studies undertaken between the 1960s and the 1980s, based on a statistical relationship (called a regression), with test scores caused by different school resources and measures of family background. These results summarize the effects of various school resources on test scores, either positive, negative, or statistically insignificant (indistinguishable from zero). Readers should come up with their interpretations of why these particular resources, including expenditures per pupil, have such weak effects on learning.

Table 3.1. Summary of Coefficients from 187 Studies of Educational Production Functions

Input	Number of Studies	Statistically Significant			Statistically Insignificant		Unknown Sign
		+	−	Total	+	−	
Teacher/pupil ratio	152	14	13	125	34	46	45
Teacher education	113	8	5	100	31	32	37
Teacher experience	140	40	10	90	44	31	15
Teacher salary	69	11	4	54	16	14	24
Expenditures/pupil	65	13	3	49	25	13	11
Administrative inputs	61	7	1	53	14	15	24
Facilities	74	7	5	62	17	14	31

Source: Hanushek (1989), table 3, p. 379.

TOOL 3-C: A RESOURCE AUDIT OF YOUR SCHOOL

Schools often undergo *fiscal audits* of their budgets, to make sure that expenditures are legitimate and comply with various restrictions on how certain revenues can be spent. But budgets describe only revenues and spending per pupil, so at best they can describe simple resources, and sometimes compound resources; but they never include complex or abstract resources, or the contributions to schooling outcomes made by students and parents. The following *resource audit* is intended to help schools account for which powerful resources they have, and which are missing.

The resources included in this audit are, with some exceptions, resources where evidence exists that they are effective in enhancing student outcomes. Some of the evidence comes from W. Norton Grubb, *The Money Myth*, especially chapter 2; other evidence comes from studies of various reform efforts. A particular school might want to use other evidence, including that generated by its experience; but whatever the source, the school should worry about the quality of the evidence. Obviously, there may be other resources that should be included; this audit should be used only as a guide to a school's deliberations.

Simple Resources

1. What is the average pupil-teacher ratio in this school? What are the highest and lowest pupil-teacher ratios? Why does variation exist?

2. How many adults are there in the school who work with students—adults including all specialists, counselors, etc.—as distinct from teachers? What is the student/adult ratio, and how does it differ by grade level, types of students, etc.?

3. What is the average teacher experience level in the school? The proportion of teachers in their first two years of teaching? The proportion of teachers with emergency credentials? How does teacher experience vary by grade, by groups of students, and by grade level, for gateway classes?

4. Which classes or groups of students have aides? How are aides prepared? What do they spend their time doing?

5. What is the student-counselor ratio in the school? Does it vary by grades or groups of students? How much of their time do counselors spend on administrative tasks (enrolling in and changing courses, etc.), academic counseling, personal counseling, and future-oriented counseling, including college and career counseling?

6. How is the time of other specialists—school psychologists, music or art teachers, curriculum coaches, etc.—distributed among students? How do they spend their time?

7. Are there any differentials or imbalances in spending per pupil for materials, books, computers, etc.?

Compound Resources

8. Have there been efforts to reduce class sizes in certain grades, courses, or for certain groups of students? What additional professional development has been give to teachers in smaller classes? What facilities have been required to accommodate smaller classes?

9. Is there adequate staff development for new teachers? (What might "adequate" mean?) For teachers adopting new curricula or materials? For teachers involved in other innovations like team teaching, pathways, or pedagogical changes?

10. Are there explicit or implicit tracks within your school? Do they affect the curricula? Teacher expectations? Student ambitions?

11. What resources are being wasted because of an inability to find complementary resources, such as space, professional development, or an adequate supply of strong candidates?

Complex Resources

12. Which teachers have control of their curricula, and which are required to use a specified curriculum? (Who chose that curriculum?) How much freedom do they have to modify the curriculum?

13. Which of your teachers are teaching outside their field of preparation?

14. How do teachers use their time? What proportion is spent on lecture? On administrative tasks? On discipline? On group work? On individual or small-group projects?

15. Does the school (or departments in high schools) encourage innovation? How do they do that? What kinds of innovation have been adopted in the past few years?

16. In observing classes, which of your teachers have mastered the methods of Direct Instruction? Which have moved toward more constructivist/conceptual/student-centered teaching? Which are balanced in their use of various approaches?

17. Think about your best and your weakest teachers. How do you judge who are good teachers versus weak teachers?

    • How are strong and weak teachers allocated? By grade levels? By specific courses? By groups of students?
    • What is the school doing to improve the instruction of the weakest teachers?

18. How much planning time do teachers have individually? What common planning time is there for groups of related teachers?

19. What does professional development for teachers look like? How much of it is "external"—outside experts providing lectures and workshops, or working with teachers on-site—and how much is "internal"—developing teacher learning communities that work on various instructional issues?

20. Similar questions about basic approaches and pedagogy could be asked of other school personnel. For example, what's the basic approach or "pedagogy" of counselors?

    • What is the pedagogy of any computer-based instruction or multimedia efforts? What's the pedagogy of the discipline system?

21. Has the school engaged in any kind of restructuring recently—for example, creating houses, or pathways, or schools-within-schools? How do these affect instruction or the personalization of the school?

Abstract Resources

22. Stability: What is the turnover rate among teachers?

    • What is the turnover rate among students? What causes this turnover, and how much could be reduced by district policy?
    • Has your school experienced changes in principals in the past few years? What policies have been changed by the new principal(s)?
    • Has the district experienced turnover in superintendents over the past few years? What policies have been changed by new superintendents?

23. School climate: Does the school take any steps to learn about student perceptions? What do these reveal?

    • What is the incidence on campus of fights? Gang-related activity? Drug or alcohol use?

24. Leadership: How do principals and assistant principals spend their time? This might determine how much time is spent on

reports to the district, reports to other groups, discipline, instruction, facilities and maintenance, etc.

- What roles do principals and assistant principals play in instruction?
- What groups of councils or teams within the school make decisions about discipline? About hiring? About curricula? About budgeting and other resource decisions? What roles do teachers play on these teams?

25. Collaboration: What groups of teachers work with one another? Are their meetings regular and scheduled, or episodic and unscheduled?

26. Trust: What are the relationships among adults in the school like? Are there groups of teachers who are not on good terms with other teachers? With members of the administration?

27. Coherence: List the different reform programs within the school, including various interventions for different subjects and grade levels; instructional improvement efforts, after-school, zero-period, and Saturday programs; and efforts by community-based organizations and other outside groups. Do these programs have anything in common except the fact that they operate at your school? Do they, for example, share an instructional philosophy, or focus on certain students, or have particular goals in mind?

CHAPTER FOUR

GOVERNMENT POLICY AND ITS EFFECTS ON CLASSROOMS AND SCHOOLS

M ANY OUTSIDE INFLUENCES affect schools and classrooms, particularly government policy. Teachers who want to play important roles in shaping their own classrooms and reforming their schools need to be aware of these external influences. The policy arena is broad and deep; therefore this chapter provides information about various levels of policy so that readers can understand the multiple forces at work, all with effects in classrooms. Understanding the way policy works will help all teachers understand better what happens to their classrooms and schools and why. Better understanding is also a precondition for teachers to participate in policy discussions—for example, in taking positions in their unions or disciplinary associations on proposed state and federal policies, or participating in district committees. By understanding policy, teachers and leaders can learn what to ask of district policy, or what positions on state policy would best support their school-level efforts. In this chapter, then, we examine the role of policies coming from districts, from states, and from the federal government. Textbox 4.1 provides some

TEXTBOX 4.1: SOURCES OF INFORMATION ABOUT POLICY

Education Week has a section on state policy as well as summaries of research. The Public Education Network (PEN) publishes reports on a variety of topics, including English learners, special education, parental involvement, and state developments. *Educational Leadership,* a publication of the Association for Supervision and Curriculum Development *(ASCD)* covers thematic issues, some of which are concerned with instructional issues and some of which focus on policy. The Education Commission of the States (www.ecs.org) collects information about a variety of state policies, often useful for comparing policies across states; the National Governors Association (www.nga.org) and the National Conference of State Legislatures (www.ncsl.org) cover a wide variety of policy issues including education. Information about federal policies is available from the U.S. Department of Education (www.ed.gov), with links to information about specific legislation, publications, and data. In addition, most states have newsletters and information centers that provide information specifically on that state. For all these official sources of information, be careful about potential bias: no government agency is likely to criticize its own policies.

sources of information about policy, though there are usually other sources for specific states.

POLICY INSTRUMENTS, THEORIES OF ACTION, AND IMPLEMENTATION PROBLEMS

Policies that originate outside schools operate in different ways than do the inner workings of a classroom or a school. Teachers influence their students directly, through how they teach, what they teach (even if that is dictated by others), and by the relationships they establish within the classroom. In contrast, districts affect children and learning not directly but indirectly, by establishing mechanisms that cause schools and teachers to act in different ways. When, for example, a district tries to improve teaching by establishing a program of professional development, it creates activities for teachers that presumably improve their instructional abilities, but the success of the policy depends on how teachers respond. When a state imposes a test-based accountability system, it provides incentives for teachers and schools to improve learning, but the tests themselves say nothing about *how* teachers and schools are to enhance learning—this is a different question, of how to enhance the capacity of teachers to improve learning. This set of linkages can be termed *the leadership chain of effect*—from external policy to principals to teachers and into classrooms—which can affect teachers and students either positively or negatively.

In one of the most influential ways of thinking about policy, Lorraine McDonnell and Richard Elmore (1987) outline four mechanisms, or instruments, by which policymakers can influence schools. The first is various *inducements*, of which the most obvious is money to districts (or directly to schools)—funding either for the general purposes of education or, in categorical grants, for specific purposes like counselors, professional development, or textbooks. Inducements might include other rewards, such as awards for Teacher of the Year or for exemplary districts, or conversely, forms of shaming when school test scores are published or schools are labeled Program Improvement schools. Second, governments can impose *mandates* on schools and classrooms—for example, the requirement that students take a certain curriculum in order to graduate from high school, or that all students take particular exams (high school exit exams or state accountability exams), or that all teachers have a particular certification. Third, governments can engage in *capacity-building*, or improving the ability of teachers, principals, schools, or districts to provide education. Professional development for teachers and mechanisms of enhancing the abilities of principals, for example through induction programs, are capacity-building efforts, as are the programs of districts or states that identify schools in special need of improvement and then concentrate resources—money, but also attention and professional development—on these low-performing schools. Finally, governments can engage in *system-creating and system-changing* reforms, changing the providers of education and their incentives in basic ways. Initiating vouchers, or developing small schools free of the usual mandates, or encouraging or mandating certain types of institutions (continuation high schools, other forms of alternative education, or area vocational schools) might be examples of system changing. Often, however, states act to reinforce systems of local institutions, for example by requiring uniformity in curricula or a uniform accountability system (both mandates) so that all schools face the same incentives.

**Key concept
policy
instruments**

(**Policy instruments** include inducements (e.g., money); mandates or requirements; capacity-building, to improve the abilities of teachers and leaders to educate students; and system-changing reforms, changing the providers of education.)

Of course, policymakers at the district, state, or federal level can use two or more of these policy levers simultaneously. For example, schools that fail to meet state standards on accountability exams (a mandate) over several years may face reconstitution, or the requirement to change principals and (in some cases) teachers as well. Presumably this is a capacity-building requirement, effected by "cleaning house" and getting rid of weak teachers, as in the Chicago 2010 Renaissance "turnaround schools," or it may be a symbolic show of reform energy that accomplishes nothing (Malen et al. 2002; Hess 2006). Complex reforms often include multiple instruments. For example, California's Immediate Intervention/Underperforming School Program (II/USP) included *inducements* in the form of additional revenue per pupil, *mandates* for creating school instructional plans, *capacity-building* in the form of external "evaluators" or coaches to help schools develop plans, and the threat of reconstitution (presumably another inducement) if schools did not improve. All these policy mechanisms operate in impersonal and rule-bound ways, applicable to all schools or to a specific subset of schools (e.g., low-performing schools), not in the more personal and tailored ways that teachers interact with students or principals as instructional leaders work directly with teachers.

Of course, policy instruments may not be effective in achieving their goals, for any number of reasons. Inducements may be too small to cause districts or schools to change their practices substantially; this is particularly the case when governments engage in symbolic efforts without enough money to make a difference—what one observer has labeled "piddle policy." Mandates may be ignored, particularly if there are no mechanisms of enforcement, or schools or districts may follow the letter but not the spirit of mandates, for example when II/USP schools developed reform plans but then did not use them. Mandates without capacity-building are particularly likely to be ineffective. No Child Left Behind contains plenty of inducements and mandates to improve the test scores of low-performing students, but the extent of capacity-building has been weak, and instead some states and districts have required scripted and semiscripted curricula that cannot possibly enhance learning—indeed, they undermine learning. System-changing efforts may fail to change existing practices; for example, although choice schools and charter schools have been promoted by some states and districts to expand the variety of schools from which parents can choose, many of these schools look a great deal like traditional schools (as we noted in Chapter 1). In the Chicago redesign supervised by now–secretary of education Arne Duncan, for example, the district planned to close 60 schools between 2004 and 2010 and open 100 new schools as small, charter, or contract schools. But these changes undermined neighborhood schools and led to a spike in school violence, disgruntled low-income parents, and destabilized communities. In the name of capacity-building, a fundamentally undemocratic approach reduced the representation of low-income communities of color—in this case bypassing the Local School Councils, which had demonstrated effective outcomes in 144 Chicago schools (Brown, Gutstein, and Lipman 2009). If teachers understand how such policies operate, they can ask appropriate questions and listen for certain responses when a district comes knocking on their doors. (See also Chapter 5 and its critique of top-down school reforms.)

Either explicitly or implicitly, every policy has a *theory of action* that asserts why it should attain its desired goals, and it is important for teachers to understand this language as a way of participating in policy conversations. A theory of action, a powerful idea articulated by Chris Argyris and Donald Schon (1978), is a conception of why a particular action should have a desired effect, given information about what influences an outcome like student learning, or persistence rather than dropout. *Espoused* theories of action are those that individuals and institutions articulate to themselves and to others when asked why a particular action or policy should have an effect; in the Chicago example, the district said reconstitution would improve outcomes for students by replacing weak leaders and teachers with stronger personnel. Often, however, policymakers have *theories in use* implied by their behavior but unconscious or poorly articulated; in Chicago the theory in use was that charter schools, without the need to hire credentialed teachers, could hire more effective and energetic teachers who had not gone through credentialing programs and who would produce better results. Among proponents of class size reduction, the conventional *theory in use* relies on the greater amount of individual attention a teacher might give his or her students in smaller classes, though a little thought suggests that a careful *espoused theory* would include many more potential effects and perhaps unintended consequences—some of which (like teaching differently in smaller classes) would require additional professional development, whereas others (a reduced ability of students to "hide out") assume that teachers are monitoring their students constantly. Tool 4-A provides an exercise in thinking about theories of action, and how carefully they outline the causal mechanisms between any policy or action and a desired outcome.

A policy initiative without a clear theory of action, or one that is based on mistaken assumptions, is unlikely to have any effect except by accident, or it may in some cases be disruptive. In Chicago, reconstituting schools without a coherent theory of action also caused "collateral damage" like increases in school violence, loss of neighborhood schools and accessibility to schools, long walks for some students, as well as job loss for some adult workers. In this chapter we will continually ask whether particular district or state policies have adequate theories of action. When we turn to school reform efforts in the next chapter, we will again ask whether particular reforms have theories of action that promote the right kind of school change.

Focus point

(A **theory of action** is a conception of why a particular action should have a desired effect. Espoused theories of action are carefully articulated to others by reformers; **theories in use**, though implied by actions, are usually less well articulated or even unconscious.)

Key concepts
theory of action
and theory in use

In addition, any policy can fail because of the implementation problem. As originally formulated by Jeffrey Pressman and Aaron Wildavsky (1979), the underlying issue is that policymakers and officials in Washington, or in state capitals, are far away from the classrooms they are trying to change. Between the original intention (or espoused theory of action) and the classroom, there are many intermediate bureaucrats and educators who have the power to veto, or hold up, or even change the intention of any policy—bureaucrats who write regulations, superintendents who may not agree with a policy change, traditional unions that resist new responsibilities for their members, principals who don't know how to change classroom practices, and teachers who fail to change their long-developed approaches. (Policy-making in the conventional approach to implementation is a top-down policy—"great expectations in Washington dashed in Oakland," in Pressman and Wildavsky's title; we will present a very different school-centered and in-side-out approach to reform in Chapter 5.) For example, No Child Left Behind intended through its funding and mandates to have "highly qualified teachers" in all classrooms. But the interpretation of "highly qualified teachers" by existing state licensing standards undermined the pressure for teacher improvement, and the implementation of accountability via basic skills tests of reading and math reduced the emphasis on subjects not being taught and thereby narrowed the curriculum. With inadequate funding and negligible increases in capacity-building despite huge new demands on schools, the policy reduced the effectiveness of teachers and the intent of NCLB, and it is so far impossible to detect any effects on learning (Fuller et al. 2007).

Focus point

The implementation problem is caused by middle- and lower-level bureaucrats and educators changing policies articulated in national and state capitals, so that they no longer meet their intended goals.

Schools are awash in policy influences from district, state, and federal levels, even if teachers and leaders do not immediately connect those influences to their daily work. This relationship offers another reason why common statements about schooling, like "it's all about people," are at best incomplete. Instead, schools are about people behaving within communities of practice *and* the policy context that they occupy. Teachers and students are like the innermost layers of an onion, or a set of Russian nested dolls: the other layers of influence are multiple, and anyone understanding a school needs to work through the outer layers of policy and influence to get to the innermost workings of the classroom. If teachers know how policy moves from the outside into the schoolhouse, they can be both more aware and more critical respondents. In the remainder of this chapter we will examine in turn district, state, and federal policy, partly to ask which of these policies support teachers and their efforts to build collective schools, and partly to see what teachers might expect of policy at different levels.

THE RANGE OF DISTRICT POLICIES

Some history is necessary to understand school districts. In the early twentieth century, when traditional approaches to schools were developing, districts were important because they had taxing authority and control over funding. In addition, the "administrative progressives" who dominated thinking about schooling focused on efficiency and the elimination of waste, on uniformity and standardization as part of creating *systems* of schools (Tyack 1974)—and districts were responsible for ensuring uniformity and efficiency. The legacy from that period, at least in traditional schools, has been an emphasis on district-wide standardization (the dreaded "one size fits all"), top-down mandates from the district, and administrative rather than instructional concerns among district officials and principals.

However, in imagining what districts *could* be, teachers and leaders might think about how they would like *schools* to act. Top-down actions by districts cause some of the waste we identified in Chapter 3. School needs and desires are often neglected in favor of district-wide curricular adoptions that sometimes generate unwanted (and often unused) textbooks and ineffective professional development; instructional improvements have either been low on district priority lists or inconsistent in implementation. Districts have often concentrated on choosing what they consider appropriate curricula, providing professional

development during the first year for the "new adoption,"
and then failing to align that training with former or current curricula or instruction, thereby conveying mixed
messages. Much of the waste in California's efforts to help
low-performing schools came from conflicts between district decisions and school development, including districts
"volunteering" schools unready for reform; the imposition
of district requirements for curricula, teacher hiring, and
consultants; and the failure of districts to provide the additional funding required by the state. Districts often don't
know how much they are spending in specific schools and
on particular programs, much less how to spend money
well (Roza and Hill 2006); and if districts don't know
much about their own spending and resources, it's difficult to know how principals and site councils can allocate
resources more effectively in the ways we outlined in
Chapter 3. Such unilateral district policies are contrary to
the notions that school changes should emphasize instructional improvements, and that they should be governed in
ways that stress internal collaboration and cooperation
rather than top-down mandates.

A number of apparently exemplary districts have acted
in ways that reflect at the *district* level how collective
schools behave. Three high-performing districts in California developed a balance between centralized policies
and decentralized or school control—the district version
of distributed leadership, with a role for schools to play in
district decision-making. They also developed processes
that allowed for shared learning among schools (Springboard Schools 2006). Similarly, in Long Beach, a district
with a reputation for innovation, schools received more
authority under the past few superintendents, developing
a balance between a top-down and a bottom-up approach; the district has engaged in wider discussion of
issues, also an element of distributed leadership. The district developed a series of interventions—a K–3 reading
initiative, an eighth-grade initiative, and a high school
program for ninth graders testing below grade level—

using a process of piloting changes and consulting with stakeholders, including schools, before enacting reforms (Austin et al. 2006). The district also brought together all members of the community and its organizations, developing the kind of "civic capacity" in which all community organizations support public schools (Stone et al. 2001). (See also the sections on rational approaches to reform in Chapter 5.) Perhaps teachers did not experience complex changes as neatly as we have laid them out here, but the effort represented a better balance between the district and schools in decision-making.

In general, districts able to respond to state policies depend on their capacity to learn new policy ideas, which in turn depend on relationships of trust and collaboration within a district and on district willingness to engage in problem-solving rather than controlling power. Similarly, a study of district responses to state accountability found that more effective "enterprising districts" worked more actively with schools, got to know individual schools well enough to understand their strengths and weaknesses, and again served as problem-solvers. "Slacking" districts, in contrast, were unable to make much progress in improving schools because they used the same approaches for all schools—the dreaded "one size fits all" (Spillane and Thompson 1997).

A second characteristic of reformed districts is a shift toward capacity-building in their schools and away from mandates. The study by Springboard Schools stressed the importance of districts focusing on instructional improvement rather than administrative issues, showing how district officials as well as principals can be instructional leaders. These districts also emphasized building capacity at the *school* level, especially through professional development to enhance teaching, as we suggested in Chapter 2. One of the districts' responsibilities was to create consistent interventions in all schools; these generally focused on developing comprehensive teaching strategies to move more students toward proficiency on state tests, rather than adopting drill-oriented curricula off the shelf or using random and fragmented interventions. Districts also followed a practice of rotating principals and administrators among positions every five years or so, in order for these individuals to develop *district*-wide perspectives, a parallel to creating teacher-leaders with schoolwide perspectives who can then become school leaders.

Districts can also support schools with certain resources, especially abstract resources—like human resources and how personnel assignments are made. Leadership stability is one such resource: districts sometimes contribute to instability by rotating principals too quickly, or by promoting assistant principals into open principal positions (often in the most difficult schools) after only two years, or by assigning assistant principals to handle discipline so they gain no experience in the other dimensions of leadership (especially instructional leadership). Teacher assignment policies also may contribute to instability if union seniority rules impede schools from hiring the teachers they want, rather than teachers reassigned from other schools—who are almost always the teachers no one wants (an assignment process sometimes called the "dance of the lemons"). The (in)coherence of a school's programs may be due partly to district policy, when districts require schools to develop many little add-on programs without any thought to the coherence of the school (Newmann et al. 2001); such a "Christmas tree approach," with bright shiny baubles (special programs) hanging on rotten branches (core teaching and the school's culture), is surely less effective than using the same money to support basic instructional capacity, leadership abilities, and the reorganization of a school into a more collegial learning community.

Another tactic in a few large urban districts has been to develop "zones," or "districts-within-districts," where consistently low-performing schools are grouped for special treatment. In Miami, these schools receive additional district support, including school observations; additional resources, including a longer day and year; specific interventions aimed at reading and math; additional teacher training; instructional coaches; mentors for inexperienced principals; and a 20 percent pay raise for teachers (Gewertz 2007). The Miami approach concentrates on resources that (perhaps with the exception of a longer day and year) are arguably effective, given the findings in Chapter 3, rather than relying on conventional practices that are expensive but ineffective, like class size reduction or traditional staff development.

Finally, a number of districts have developed school-based budgeting (SBB), in which districts allocate a certain fraction of district revenue to schools to spend as they see fit. Such practices follow the logic that *schools* must have the ability to determine what resources are developed if they are to be responsible for improving learning. Many (but not all) districts that have adopted SBB have used weighted student formulas in allocating funds, where schools with higher proportions of low-income students, English learners, and students with disabilities receive more money. There are often different weights for different levels of the schooling, and sometimes different weights for specific programs like vocational education or gifted-and-talented programs. One of the main concerns SBB attempts to address is equity among schools, and school-based budgeting (especially in conjunction with weighted student formulas) does in fact improve the equity of funding per student among schools.

However, SBB is potentially important not only for its equity effects but also because it provides schools with new incentives to become more effective. Rather than allocating only a small discretionary fund for the principal, SBB gives new responsibilities to principals, and usually to school-site councils, to make resource decisions with more substantial sums of money. This provides a new incentive to think about the resources schools might want and how to use their available funds to create those resources. From

the perspective of Chapter 3 and its concern with resources, the real promise of SBB is that it might lead principals and other participants (teacher-leaders and
school-site council members) in school-level planning to
become more expert at diagnosing educational problems,
determining effective ways of resolving them, and then—
because they have the funding to do so—implementing
real solutions. (See Tool 4-B for this approach to budgeting and resources, a process that can be valuable in all
schools with some discretion over spending as well as in
schools with SBB.) Technical assistance to principals and
school budget committees, and steady improvements in
SBB procedures, could result in leaders and teachers who
are better able to make effective resource decisions.

Overall, then, innovative districts can support collective schools in many ways. Teachers and their schools
might expect their districts to operate in more open and
collaborative ways, responding to school needs rather
than imposing reforms that may not match individual
schools, their histories, and their decisions. Support for
capacity-building, so that schools have the ability to
meet state and federal mandates, is another characteristic
of supportive rather than authoritarian district policies.
Even if districts do not move all the way to school-based
budgeting, they can at least allocate money and other resources to support effective practices. And for teachers
and teacher-leaders, understanding how policy levers operate gives them more information and potential influence over decisions that directly affect their schools.

STATES AND CAPACITY-BUILDING

When public schools were first established, states played
only a small role in funding them (i.e., providing inducements). Gradually, however, shortages of funds from local property taxes (particularly during periodic recessions
and the Great Depression) caused state funding to increase, and pressures for equity among districts also led

to increases in state revenues. Currently, states provide 48 percent of all school funding, though this proportion varies widely from almost 90 percent in Hawaii to 27 percent in Nevada. A great deal of this support comes in the form of categorical grants, which support only limited purposes. These grants are a barrier to districts and schools that would like to use funds flexibly.

With increased state funding has come more state control—another illustration of the Golden Rule: he (or she) who has the gold makes the rules. Currently, states impose a large number of requirements on districts and schools, including high school graduation requirements, curriculum standards, teacher and principal credentialing, lists of approved textbooks, state accountability mechanisms, and high school exit exams. In effect, many states have assumed that they can improve schools through these mandates. This kind of top-down policy is behaviorist in all its assumptions—that districts and schools respond to rewards and punishments, just as rats in laboratories do.

Recently, however, states have started to develop more effective forms of capacity-building:

- Professional development aimed at teachers, including induction and coaching. The effectiveness of such efforts depends on careful implementation. One example is Kentucky's Highly Skilled Educator model, where selected experienced teachers assist schools in implementing state standards, supported by members of a regional team. Preliminary results suggest that this approach is effective only in conjunction with other reforms—an example of a compound resource.
- External consultants to low-performing schools. These teams collect data and propose "doable strategies with specific timelines and targets" that the school community must then approve.

Most seem to follow the technical-rational approach to reform we outline in Chapter 5. How well the external consultants and teams work is unclear, though careful preparation of mentors, as Kentucky provides, and constant evaluation and improvement of these programs could make them more effective over time.

- Continuous improvement loops to help low-performing schools. Individual schools generate data to examine areas of low performance, improve teaching and learning in the areas of greatest need, and evaluate the results as input into another round of analysis and improvement. These are also examples of rational approaches to school reform.

- Additional funding for low-performing schools, including California's II/USP program and High Priority School Grants Program (HPSGP), described in the previous chapter. Kentucky's Commonwealth School Improvement Fund (CSIF) is another example, providing funds to improve instruction and assessment, replicate successful programs, encourage cooperation in instructional approaches, and encourage experimentation. A preliminary evaluation of CSIF indicates that it has, both by itself and in conjunction with other reforms, improved test scores by small increments (Legislative Research Commission 2006, table 4.2).

- Tiered systems identifying schools *and* districts in need of special attention, with low-performing schools and districts receiving more technical assistance or additional funding. In addition, six states have won waivers under No Child Left Behind for pilot projects in which they focus resources on schools in the worst shape (Zuckerbrod 2008).

These capacity-building efforts are quite different from the traditional state policies of funding, categorical programs, and requirements. Implicitly, they assume that money isn't the only thing that matters. Instead they focus on the quality of instruction, and in some cases school and district leadership, rather than on conventional credentials; they often use the expertise of experienced teachers and administrators to improve practices. They promote highly rationalist practices—data analysis, reliance on methods shown to be effective, continuous improvement processes in place of the haphazard and fragmented decisions that many schools and districts have followed—which have upsides and downsides, discussed in Chapter 5.

Focus point

One other possibility for states has not yet been developed. Chapter 3 clarified the importance of teachers, leaders, and their districts knowing as much as possible about *effective* resources. There are substantial economies of scale in collecting such information at the state rather than the district or school level, and doing so might make state policymakers more aware of effectiveness and less prone to passing legislation that is well intentioned but ineffective. But state agencies are far away from the classroom and do not fully understand how policy affects students; teachers and leaders are in better positions to understand the details of "what works" at the school level. *If states could gather research evidence about effective practice, incorporating the experience that school-level educators have, this broad evidence could replace the limited and top-down model of the What Works Clearinghouse. Teachers and school leaders would also have an avenue for questioning and participating in policy.* Such an approach to evidence is consistent with the school-centered, inside-out approach to reform we develop in Chapter 5.

Focus point

The effectiveness of state capacity-building is not yet clear, for these programs are too new to have been carefully evaluated (Calkins et al. 2007). When states have little ability to learn from their errors—as in California, which has ignored the negative results of class size reduction and multibillion-dollar efforts to help low-performing schools—then state policy has little chance of improving, and states simply add to waste in the system. When states evaluate their efforts seriously—as Kentucky has done with its various reforms—and then make adjustments, more effective state policies can emerge. When teachers can understand and contribute to the evidence underlying state policy, they are in a better position to further state objectives. (See Textbox 4.1 for some teacher-friendly sources about policy.) Not every teacher (especially beginning teachers) will take an interest in state policy and implementation, but those who do contribute both to policy-making and to the knowledge of their peers about what influences classrooms.

THE SCHIZOPHRENIC FEDERAL ROLE

Teachers generally know there is something amiss with federal policy, and this section tries to acquaint them with enough history and current developments to explain why. Federal aid for education began with legislation in 1864 providing grants of land for states to establish public universities (now the flagship universities in most states), and to the Smith-Hughes Act of 1917, which provided federal aid for vocational education. The "modern" era of federal aid dates to the 1960s, when Lyndon Johnson's War on Poverty emphasized schooling and training to help individuals escape poverty. Many of the current federal programs were created then: the Elementary and Secondary Education Act, reauthorized every five years and now in the form of No Child Left Behind; Head Start for prekindergarten education; and Job Corps and job training programs outside the educational system, continued in the current Workforce Investment Act. All of these focused on different aspects of equity and inclusion, and this pattern has persisted in more recent federal aid for bilingual education and for students with disabilities.

Unfortunately, the consequences of federal efforts have been highly uncertain. The effectiveness of Title I—the 1965 act to improve academic achievement of the disadvantaged—has always been contentious, as have the appropriate programs for English learners (Vinovskis 1999; Farkas and Hall 2000; Puma et al. 1997; Minow 1997; Hakuta and Cancino 1977). Special education policy was instituted in 1975 with the Individuals with Disabilities Education Act (IDEA), which has been reauthorized every five years since then. Although the inclusiveness of IDEA has benefited some students enormously, the act has also created funding problems by requiring more of districts and schools than the funds it provides, resulting in the difficult condition of "unfunded mandates." But even worse, it has often been a dumping ground where the most "difficult" and disruptive students, often students of color who come from low-income families, are relegated to weak programs with underequipped classrooms and a shortage of qualified teachers, where they "experience inadequate services, low-quality curriculum and instruction, and unnecessary isolation from their non-disabled peers" (Losen and Orfield 2002). With some important exceptions, federal aid for vocational education has funded highly traditional approaches emphasizing preparation for low-level jobs, creating yet another "dumping ground" in many schools. There's no question that federal funding has supported some effective local programs, but—between the fact that federal spending has been only 8 percent of K–12 spending and the conclusion that federal practices have often promoted ineffective efforts—it remains unclear whether federal efforts on the whole have narrowed inequalities or not, despite the commitment of all major federal legislation to equity.

This uncertainty continues in No Child Left Behind, particularly because the rhetoric of federal efforts has not been matched by the funding or other resources necessary to enhance school capacity. The crucial question, being hotly debated as reauthorization of NCLB is imminent, is whether it has helped or hindered equity, in any sense of the term. Most obviously, as for state accountability systems, the pressures of NCLB—and especially the need to make Annual Yearly Progress toward the absolute goal of having all groups of students score at the "proficient" level by 2014—have made educators acutely aware of low-performing students. Most schools understand their status under NCLB and are trying frantically to improve test scores; the efforts of districts and states, varied though they may be, have also been driven by NCLB requirements.

For some advocates, the articulation of uniform standards for all students and all subgroups of students is enough to buy allegiance to NCLB. But the equitable intentions of NCLB are not matched by the detail of its requirements, and it has worked in complex and (perhaps) unintended ways. It has increased the pressure to increase test performance quickly, and pressure for immediate results has caused many states, districts, and schools to adopt off-the-shelf programs of doubtful value, quick fixes in place of the longer-run process of enhancing teacher capacity. It has narrowed the focus to English and math, and within these subjects to those elements that are readily tested—vocabulary and simple comprehension rather than deeper understanding, and mastery of arithmetic procedures rather than mathematical reasoning. In all too many schools, NCLB has led to narrow efforts to teach to the test, to triage practices focusing on "bubble kids" on the cusp of proficiency, and sometimes to cheating. Despite early promises of substantially increased funding, federal revenues have not increased to meet the additional demands of NCLB, leaving districts (especially urban districts) in the position of having to come up with additional revenues—the problem of "unfunded mandates" again. Politicians, including George Bush, have been quick to call on schools to prepare students for "a constantly changing world that is demanding increasingly complex skills from its workforce," and many commissions and employers have called on schools to increase rigor and standards. But low-performing students in basic skills interventions prompted by NCLB are not likely to be well prepared for the demands of the future workforce or for responsible citizenship, but only for more low-level tests—which have little to do with other meaningful goals.

Furthermore, whereas the information on effective practices could be a national responsibility (again because of economies of scale), the Bush administration's approach to this role was unhelpful and even counterproductive. The What Works Clearinghouse accumulates a variety of studies and summarizes their results about effectiveness. However, the clearinghouse has used a narrow conception of evidence, including only the statistically most sophisticated studies and ignoring all qualitative evidence. Clearinghouse reports are written for researchers rather than for principals and teachers unfamiliar with the language of research. So, though the provision of information about effective practices would be a useful role, schools trying to use the clearinghouse to select programs face severely limited information.

Overall, the well-intentioned history of federal aid doesn't support much faith in the federal efforts to improve schools. Even though few educators would be willing to lose federal funding, these efforts provide yet another illustration of how additional money may not matter that much. The shift to No Child Left Behind only continues that checkered history, with small amounts of additional funding inadequate to the additional demands placed on schools and districts, and with further distortion of how districts and schools spend their revenues. The overall ineffectiveness of Title I efforts continues in NCLB: the evidence so far indicates that NCLB has made no difference in school improvement, and Reading First has increased the time spent on reading but not reading comprehension (Fuller et al. 2007; Institute for Educational Science 2008).

What might teachers expect from federal aid to education? The focus on groups of students who are poorly served has surely been a great strength of federal policy since the 1960s. But the accomplishments of federal legislation have not matched its good intentions. Sometimes this has happened because of political disagreements— over bilingual education, for example, or over the simple accountability mechanisms and voucher-like mechanisms in NCLB. Sometimes the theories of action underlying federal practices have been inadequate, as in the long history of programs in Title I that pull students out of their regular classrooms, or the scripted and semiscripted curricula adopted under NCLB. In response, teachers and their representatives might focus on the effectiveness of federal spending, demanding that the same conceptions of effective resources developed in Chapter 3, and of effective policy developed in this chapter, be applied to federal programs.

Second, as for state policy, teachers and school leaders might demand greater support for capacity-building. At the very least, they could insist that the additional demands of federal legislation (as in NCLB and special education) be matched by capacity-building to meet those demands. Knowledge about unfunded mandates at least helps teachers understand why it is usually impossible to meet all the requirements of federal legislation; then their responsibility is to sort through the possibilities and develop feasible and productive plans. And federal capacity-building implies not only providing adequate funding but also more careful attention (as in state policies) to professional development, including induction programs to enhance the capacities of teachers and leaders. It might encompass efforts to enhance the capacities of states and their departments of education to support districts and schools.

Third, teachers and school leaders and their organizations, following the logic of Chapter 3, might ask their national, state, and local organizations to ask Washington to develop an educator-friendly version of the What Works Clearinghouse, an online resource that could be more responsive and useful for teachers and leaders at the school level. Such a clearinghouse would make it easier for schools and districts to learn about effective practices, including those with coherent theories of action, and to check whether their own ideas of "what works" are supported by any evidence. In that way, teachers can become active users of research, matching their thinking with that of experts and sharing results of their efforts with other users.

Many other federal roles could support equity, particularly the noneducational policies (examined in Chapter 6) that are complementary to public schooling—health and housing policies, community development, and the like. But the potential for federal policy in education will not be fully developed until the constituencies for equity— including teachers and their unions and disciplinary organizations—clarify which policies have been helpful and which have actually harmed the cause of equity.

TEACHER ROLES IN UNIONS AND DISCIPLINARY ASSOCIATIONS

Although teachers and teacher-leaders can participate in politics as individuals, they have more power as members of organized interest groups—unions primarily, but also a range of disciplinary organizations and other groups. All of these provide opportunities for teachers to take on leadership roles inside and outside the school. Administrators certainly view a school's "union reps" as essential members of governance structures like site councils and leadership teams, but the relationship is typically bureaucratic and more antagonistic than it needs to be—primarily because of the history of teacher unions. The union leadership role in and out of schools could be more productive if teachers as union members understood the different kinds of roles unions can play.

Unions have a complex and somewhat contradictory role within districts and schools because they take at least three forms, each with its own history: trade unions, professional unions, and social justice unions. The first teacher unions were modeled on industrial labor unions, with salaries, benefits, hours, and obligations outlined in contracts that are often bitterly negotiated (Moore et al. 2007). As a result, work rules are applied rigidly from school to school, interactions with administrators are highly ritualized and hierarchical, and roles are inflexible. The ultimate goal of industrial unions has been to protect the self-interest of workers, and the same has been true of teacher unions following this model.

But teaching is not like working in a factory, despite the egg carton architecture and rigid school schedules; teachers aren't just cogs in a machine. Instead, they develop sophisticated skills and specialized experience, and they are constantly faced with new situations and must diagnose and address unexpected problems. Unlike industrial workers, teachers share common interests and professional status with administrators, and even more so in collective schools with distributed leadership. Over time, then, the model of industrial unionism has become an inappropriate model for the work of teachers and schools. Beginning in the early 1990s a movement toward "professional unionism" developed, and the apparently contradictory motto of the American Federation of Teachers (AFT) was born: "a union of professionals." Professional unions are characterized by a focus on teacher and administrator collaboration, concern for the public interest, and the shared ownership of reform efforts between teachers and administrators. Adversarial bargaining has been replaced by more collaborative bargaining in which teachers and administrators focus on common interests and seek out agreements in which both sides get some of what they want. Whereas industrial unionism focused on protecting *teachers*, professional unionism focuses on protecting *teaching*, particularly teaching as a professional occupation based on deep knowledge and some autonomy (Kercher and Caufman 1999). This focus acknowledges the links between self-interest and the public interest; what is good for students, not just for teachers, becomes a major consideration. (See, for example, the statement from the New York chapter of the UFT in Textbox 4.2.) As a trade union, such unions continue to advocate for teachers on issues related to salary, performance pay, and benefits. As a professional union, their approach is concerned with the professional standing of teachers, particularly in their authority over curriculum and instruction. As a children's lobby, professional unions advocate for reform initiatives on such issues as school funding, class size, health care, and accountability. This reflects what union presidents referred to as a "hybrid approach" (Moore et al. 2007, 17).

There is not necessarily agreement about industrial versus professional unionism. All too often veteran teachers want to preserve the traditional role of unions—protecting teachers from administrative abuse, ensuring fair assignments, negotiating higher salaries and retirement benefits—whereas novice teachers have different expectations. Novice teachers sometimes view unions as providing them *services* in exchange for *fees*. They expect administrative support and professional development opportunities from their unions. But they also expect unions to be more flexible in their response to tenure and teacher compensation, and are more open to novel approaches like pay for performance or creating career ladders. It's difficult to know how to resolve this difference in perspectives, rooted in the very different experiences teachers of different generations have had; it may require a generational change to establish professional unions more securely. But for those who are relatively new to teaching, this rift clarifies that unions need not take only one form, and that teachers can demand that their unions represent them in different ways.

TEXTBOX 4.2: DEFINING A PROFESSIONAL UNION

"Recognizing that the interests of schoolchildren and their teachers are inseparable, the UFT (United Federation of Teachers) combines its roles as a trade union and as an influential children's lobby to help make every public school a place where parents want to send their children and where educators want to work." (From the website http://www.uft.org/about/, accessed October 6, 2009)

Key concept
social justice unionism

A hopeful trend that has emerged within the past decade is an adaptation of "professional unionism" into what advocates call "social justice unionism." **Social justice unionism** "retains the best of traditional unionism, borrows from what has been called 'professional unionism' and is informed by a broader concept of our members' self-interests and by a deeper social vision" (Peterson and Charney 1999, 129). This conception requires members to confront issues of race and class, and it more closely aligns with the roles of teacher-leaders as agents for social justice. According to the National Coalition of Education Activists, social justice unionism should (1) defend the rights of members while fighting for the rights and needs of the broader community and students; (2) incorporate parents and community members as key allies; (3) involve rank-and-file membership directly; (4) encourage teachers to address issues of racial and gender equity, racism, and prejudice in classrooms; and (5) advocate for the radical restructuring of American education.

To this we might add that social justice unions would also support those noneducational policies complementary to schooling—health and housing policies, antidiscrimination measures, income support and labor market policies—that we examine in Chapter 6. Though no social justice unions have emerged as key players in education policy and reform, elements of this approach are evident within the rhetoric, action, and history of both the AFT and the National Education Association

(NEA). In fact, the AFT has a specific "social justice" link on its website, leading to a list of past AFT actions in pursuit of social justice. This provides a resource within the larger context of unionism and other potential leadership roles for teachers.

In addition to unions, teachers and teacher-leaders belong to a variety of other associations that can serve as interest groups in the political process. These include disciplinary (or subject-matter) associations, like the National Council for the Social Studies, the National Councils of Teachers of English and of Math, and the Association for Career Technical Education. Most often, within education policy, they formulate and advocate for standards and curricula they have devised; for example, the NCTM standards have been widely followed by math instructors and textbook publishers. As service organizations they provide members with access to monthly or quarterly magazines or newsletters, professional development, yearly conferences and networking opportunities, and curricular resources. Some organizations, such as the International Reading Association, also fund and publish their own research. Other associations are organized around certain grade levels (e.g., the National Middle School Association and the National Association for the Education of Young Children) or identifiable groups of students, like the Council for Exceptional Children. Yet other groups, closer in spirit to social justice unions, advocate for a more explicit social justice agenda; these include groups like the National Council of Education Activists and the Network of Teacher Activist Groups, along with primarily local groups like Teachers 4 Social Justice (San Francisco) and the New York Collective of Radical Activists. As with disciplinary associations and grade-level groups, these organizations provide like-minded teachers with networking opportunities, professional development, and curricular resources.

There are, then, many ways for teachers to participate not only in their schools but also in the deliberations around district, state, and federal policies. These are ways to create more powerful interest groups, articulating the educational needs of children—and their noneducational needs as well—in political arenas where children cannot represent their own interests. Such associations can also project new images of teachers—as professionals dedicated to improving instruction, as advocates for particular reforms where they have as much expertise as anyone else, as educators promoting school reform from the inside out, from the school level outward (as we argue in the next chapter)—and not, as they are often portrayed, as self-interested groups blocking all change.

SOCIAL JUSTICE AND THE EQUITY PARADOX

There are, of course, many steps teachers and schools can take on their own to enhance equity, including adopting more powerful approaches to instruction, treating all students fairly, and eliminating practices like tracking that systemically redirect resources from some students to others. But equity and social justice are impossible to achieve fully at the classroom and school levels. If we think about the allocation of resources among schools, then some district, state, or federal action is necessary. If schools were left to their own resources—to the resources they could attract from the surrounding community—then schools in low-income areas of cities would have low levels of spending and of the resources that money can buy, and they would particularly suffer during recessions (including the current one), when layoffs and unemployment increase. Nonmoney resources would similarly be inadequate und uneven: high-quality or experienced teachers and leaders would flee to the suburbs, exacerbating the inequitable distribution of human resources and pedagogical approaches. We now rely primarily on states (and to a lesser extent on districts and federal practices) to correct these inequalities, and so equity requires schools to rely on district, state, and federal

Cross-Reference For a related discussion of teacher actions to improve schools, see **Book 5, Chapter 5.**

policy at the same time they remain vigilant and informed of the policies.

But here we need to confront a paradox. A great deal of policy-making is concerned with equity in some sense or another, including state equalization efforts, federal compensatory efforts, programs for "disadvantaged" students, English learners, students with disabilities, and students who have fallen behind who are the targets of interventions, after-school programs, and other efforts to boost the intensity of learning. Equity has been more or less permanently on the reform agenda since the 1960s, and the school reform "industry" has become large and pervasive (as we detail in the next chapter). There have indeed been some victories. The gap in years of schooling between white and black Americans has decreased since the 1940s, contributing to a narrowing (but obviously not an elimination) of earnings differences (Smith and Welch 1986); the racial achievement gaps in achievement measured by the National Assessment of Educational Progress and by the high school dropout rate have narrowed since the early 1970s (Magnuson and Waldfogel 2008, especially ch. 2).

But the gains of the past forty years seem small compared with the persistent inequity we face. Improvements in the achievement gap seem to have stalled since around 1990. There are many other gaps to worry about, especially the white-Latino gap both in test scores and in high school completion. The latter seems to have peaked somewhere between the mid-1950s and mid-1960s and has gotten somewhat worse since then; as the economy has fewer jobs for those without high school diplomas, and access to postsecondary education for dropouts remains difficult, the plight of dropouts has gotten worse and worse. The transition from high school to college, the most recent "crisis" to hit public education, is yet another barrier to equity, and one that—despite thousands of well-intentioned but fragmentary programs that emphasize college-going—is far from any systematic solution. In

Improvements in the achievement gap seem to have stalled since around 1990.

addition, equity is a moving target, and new developments exacerbating *inequality*—the greater earnings inequality since the 1970s, the continued immigration of
groups from many low-income countries, the enormous
inequalities after 2000 caused by unequal earnings patterns, now the fiscal crisis triggered by corporate greed
and dishonesty—are setbacks to prior successes. Social
justice has been more or less permanently on the policy
agenda, but there still doesn't seem to be much progress.

One reason is that just as there are constituencies for
equity, there are comparable—indeed stronger—
constituencies for *in*equity. Parents in high-spending
schools and districts don't want resources to be reallocated away from their children; well-resourced schools
don't want to see equalization of competent teachers,
strong leaders, supportive services, extracurricular activities, and all the other monetary and nonmonetary resources that make them effective. Even in the urban
schools to which white middle-class parents send their
children, there are inequities as some parents participate
more vocally, demanding that their children be the center of concern, assigned the better teachers, or given special (and expensive) placements within special education.
Coalitions of parents from both poorly funded and well-
funded districts have often been opponents in school finance lawsuits, and state legislatures and school boards
often defer to middle-class parents and their demands.
Parents and educators have not found ways to form
coalitions supporting stronger schools for all students;
instead we have a politics of education that pits different
interest groups against one another.

In addition, although equity has been on the political
agenda since the 1960s, there have still been cycles of attention and inattention. The War on Poverty of the 1960s
was a high point of federal legislation; federal commitment and equity began to slip away under Ronald Reagan, and then under George W. Bush, both of whom
attacked equity not only in education but in other

spheres, including tax structures, the right to unionize, employment, lending and housing, legal services, and many other government activities. Supporters of President Barack Obama kindled hope that there would be another cycle of greater attention to equity, a resurgence of the War on Poverty of the 1960s. In addition, attention to the equity agenda rises and falls with the business cycle. During a deep recession like the one that began in 2008, it is difficult to maintain many equity-related programs, and so *sustained* attention to equity programs, and *sustained* development, are frequently interrupted by the business cycle.

Finally, it's possible that real equity in education may cost more than anyone has been willing to admit—both in money and in other school resources. A program called Making Waves, which provides comprehensive supports for low-performing students in Richmond, California, spends $12,000–$13,000 per student; when this is added to the amount already provided by the district, it becomes likely that the real cost per student might be around $20,000, much more than any public school spends. Elite private schools spend in the range of $20,000–$30,000 per student, some for nonacademic enrichment but much of it for smaller classes with balanced instruction, stable teachers, and adequate facilities. Under current conditions, an adequate supply of credentialed and experienced teachers in urban districts would require much higher salaries, and many compound resources would require additional funding for several expensive components (smaller class sizes *and* professional development *and* adequate facilities). The vision, leadership, and cooperation necessary to improve low-performing schools are other desperately scarce resources that need to be increased, and it's unclear how to do that. So the resource requirements for equity may be more substantial than anyone has acknowledged, and often the only feasible programs are relatively small and inconsequential efforts—"piddle policies"—that accomplish very little.

Real equity in education may cost more than anyone has been willing to admit.

But "piddle policies" only perpetuate the educational differences among children. Furthermore, as Gloria Ladson-Billings (2006) has argued, inequalities in education are compounded over time, as differences in parental educational levels, earnings, access to health care, conventional political power, and many other resources in turn affect schooling in the next generation. *The educational variation in each generation leads to an accumulation of differences, an educational debt that grows larger year by year and that—like the national debt that increases when the country runs deficits—has become an ever larger burden to the educational system and a barrier to equitable schooling.*

Focus point

There is, unfortunately, no simple solution to these dilemmas; they are part of promoting equitable schools in a highly inequitable society. But education is one of the very few public institutions where the equity agenda is fully legitimate, where the goals of "leaving no child behind" and developing *all* of our human resources are widely accepted, and where teachers and unions and disciplinary associations are legitimately engaged in the work of social justice. With a few additional supports— the demise of the free-market rhetoric of the past thirty years, a change in the administration in Washington, and (one hopes) a turnaround in the national economy—this is an excellent moment to press the equity agenda.

DISCUSSION QUESTIONS

1. In what ways do *district* policies support your *school's* efforts to become more equitable? To become more effective? In what ways does the district limit or constrain your school's reforms, or impose its own reforms? One way to answer this question is to take a specific reform at your school and ask what the district's role has been.

2. In what ways do *state* policies support or constrain your *school's* efforts? In answering this question, you might distinguish between state efforts to fund K–12 education at particular levels and state efforts to act in nonfiscal ways to shape educational practices—that is, between state *inducements* and state *mandates.* Has your state engaged in any *capacity-building*, including efforts like those described in the section on state policies above? Again, tracing a policy from the state to the district to your school might be helpful.

3. What have been the effects of No Child Left Behind in your school and your district? Does your school receive extra funding? What have been the school's responses to the additional accountability and requirements attached to that funding (including curriculum changes)? Does the additional funding cover the additional "costs"—financial costs, learning costs, and human costs—of NCLB?

4. Of all the district, state, and federal policies affecting your school, which have been the most effective in supporting your reforms? Which would you most like to see expanded?

FURTHER READING

Argyris, Chris, and Donald Schon. 1978. *Organizational Learning: A Theory of Action Perspective.* Reading, MA: Addison-Wesley.

Calkins, Andrew, William Guenther, Grace Belfiore, and Dave Lash. 2007. *The Turnaround Challenge: Supplement to the Main Report.* Boston: Insight Education and Research Institute.

Fuller, Bruce, Joseph Wright, Karen Gesicki, and Erin Kang. 2007. "Gauging Growth: How to Judge No Child Left Behind?" *Educational Researcher* 36, 5: 268–278.

Ladson-Billings, Gloria. 2006. "From the Achievement Gap to the Education Debt: Understanding Achievement in U.S. Schools." *Educational Researcher* 35, 7: 3–12.

Pressman, Jeffery, and Aaron Wildavsky. 1979. *Implementation: How Great Expectations in Washington Are Dashed in Oakland: or, Why It's Amazing That Federal Programs Work at All, This Being a Saga of the Economic Development*

Administration as Told by Two Sympathetic Observers Who Seek to Build Morals on a Foundation of Ruined Hopes. Berkeley: University of California Press.

Stone, Clarence. 2001. *Building Civic Capacity: The Politics of Reforming Urban Schools.* Lawrence: University Press of Kansas.

TOOL 4-A: THEORIES OF ACTION

Think about the following policies, all of which have been commonly advocated as ways of enhancing student performance. What is the *espoused* theory of action underlying each one? What is the *theory in use*, or implicit theory of action, that people commonly use when they promote this policy? Be sure to clarify any assumptions necessary for these theories of action, and consider the variety of resources included in the resource audit of Tool 3-C.

Reconstituting schools by replacing leaders and (most) teachers.

Charter schools freed of most district requirements (which requirements should remain?).

Teacher aides.

Increasing the length of the school day or the school year.

Creating year-round schools.

After-school programs.

Class size reduction.

High school reforms:

    Breaking up large comprehensive high schools into smaller schools-within-schools.

    Multiple pathways with themes.

    Early-college high schools with some courses taken in community colleges.

    International Baccalaureate (IB) programs.

High-stakes exams: high school exit exams, or national exams to overcome the presumed problems of No Child Left Behind of having states set exams and standards.

What implementation problems might you expect with each of these policies?

TOOL 4-B: A BUDGETING PROCESS BASED ON INSTRUCTIONAL IMPROVEMENT

Many if not most schools spend their discretionary funds piecemeal, particularly if they receive categorical grants (grants that can be spent only on a specific category of resources, like computers, books, or guidance counselors) from the state or foundations. In districts with student-based budgeting, where districts allocate large sums of money to schools to spend as they see fit, there is usually little preparation in how to think about budgets, expenditures, and effective resources. The alternative is to plan a budget so that it supports the school's educational needs, considering a wider variety of resources. One procedure to do so is this:

1. Examine the waste in your school, as in Tool 3-A. What possibilities do these sources of waste suggest for reallocating resources within the school?

2. Carry out a comprehensive survey of the school's existing resources, as in the resource audit of Tool 3-C.

3. Identify the current patterns of educational outcomes among students. These should not be limited to standardized tests but incorporate other measures of learning, of progress through schools including students retained in grade or (in high school) credits accumulated, disciplinary actions, and student attitudes like educational ambitions. The school should identify particular needs and rank them in some way to get a sense of priorities.

4. Identify what reforms would help address each of these education needs. (Be sure to clarify the theories of action underlying these reforms.) Because the needs have been prioritized, the reforms should already be prioritized.

5. Identify what resources are necessary for each of the reforms. "Resources" are broadly defined as in Chapter 3 and include not only money for specific activities (release time, professional development, etc.) but also administrative attention and leadership, teacher cooperation, district support, instructional

improvement, and other complex and abstract resources. Note that the wasted resources identified in step 1 should be available to be reallocated. The fiscal resources necessary for these reforms then are included in fiscal budgets; the nonmonetary resources clarify where the time and attention of teachers and leaders should be concentrated.

If these stages are periodically updated, then the school can be ready with its spending and resource priorities whenever new funding or other resources come along.

TOOL 4-C: THE CONSTITUENCIES FOR EDUCATIONAL REFORM

For your *district* and then your *state*, identify some of the prominent education policies currently being considered. Who (or which districts or which groups of educators) are in favor of them? Who is against them? What do these alignments reveal about different conceptions of *effectiveness*? About different conceptions of *equit'y*?

- Commission Reports, Frameworks, and Strategic Plans

- Taking Charge of Reform

- Reasonable, Rational Approaches to Reform

- Evidence-Based Practice

- Social Justice and School Reform

CHAPTER FIVE

TEACHER PARTICIPATION IN MULTIPLE FORMS OF SCHOOL REFORM

PILOT PROJECTS, scaling up, cycles of inquiry, theories of action, change theory, implementation issues, unintended consequences. School reform follows a familiar pattern. A reform emerges, gains currency, is tried in a few schools, is authorized as effective—and bingo, disappears. The sequence is predictable: first comes the energy for developing a reform, followed by "selling" the project to district or school leaders, then funding for professional development and implementation—all too often with limited support in the classroom—and, last, documentation of results. Four or five years later that project is forgotten, the materials are on a shelf somewhere, and the school or district moves on to some other promising idea.

The publication of *A Nation at Risk* in 1983 ushered in the modern era of school reform. (See Tool 5-A to examine the language and influence of the report.) Hundreds of nonprofit organizations now offer districts a specific reform model that is injected into schools almost like an immunization. Foundations develop or guide school reform according to their funding focus; for example, the Gates Foundation offered funding to small autonomous schools, and the Fisher Foundation (of the GAP stores) funds KIPP schools. School reform is an industry of planners, policymakers, implementation experts, consultants, and evaluators—some private, some nonprofit, and some public. Nearly every school has pilot projects or grant funds for small initiatives; some schools are even compared to Christmas trees with dozens of bright shiny reform initiatives. Whatever its strengths and weaknesses, the school reform movement has energy and resources, but uneven success. Often the results have been, as David Tyack and Larry Cuban (1995) describe it, "tinkering toward utopia" without developing a reasonable approach to solutions. This chapter draws on their analysis and also offers several key recommendations for how teachers and leaders in the collective school can do more than tinker.

In the quarter century since *A Nation at Risk* was published, several stages of large-scale reform emerged and were touted as successes. Competency-based curricula and the effective schools research of the early 1980s led to massive efforts to engage states in developing standards. George H. W. Bush's Thousand Points of Light followed, with federally funded comprehensive school reform authorizing certain initiatives to replicate themselves, or in reform-ese to "scale up." By 2002, high-stakes accountability, premised on the largely discredited Texas miracle and based on multiple-choice tests, had taken hold. Now a reexamination of that approach, with its one-size-fits-all testing, is occurring because No Child Left Behind hasn't worked well for many schools. This pattern of reform poses obvious questions: What could durable change look like in a school? How could different *school-centered and teacher-generated* approaches to reform increase student engagement and learning? How can teacher-leaders and administrators jointly engage in efforts that promote both depth and longevity of reform?

Often, however, teachers and students get lost in the reform mix. Particularly in urban schools, teachers and students are often the objects—but rarely the initiators—of varied district, state, and federal initiatives and foundation efforts. The "tinkering" is in the hands of outside "mechanics," whereas the appropriate drivers of the reform are the recipients, not the agents. The entire operation has the feel of what Stan Karp (2003) calls "drive-by" reforms: proposals for change are generated from outside the school; the school becomes the wary "target of intervention," with lip service to teacher participation; the reform is typically disconnected from the school's history; and implementation timelines, trotted out by experts, offer outside professional development, rather than the more effective types of internal professional development we outlined in Chapter 2.

In this chapter we suggest alternatives for teachers and teacher-leaders—and for the administrators wrestling with reforms. Our premise, as we have stated throughout this book, is that teachers have a pivotal role to play in everything about schooling, and we offer a school-based alternative that supports change efforts from inside the school. In this approach, teachers and teacher-leaders play critical roles because only they have the deep knowledge of a school and its students, of its history and previous reform efforts. Only they can determine if a particular reform can really work in that school; only they can act from the inside out.

However, teachers must first understand the methods and language of reform. Knowledge is power, and they can only participate meaningfully by understanding the language and perspectives that researchers, reformers, and consultants have developed: change theory, theories of action, and trustworthy evidence. They need a grasp of action research or cycles of inquiry and a plan for engaging in the process of change more effectively. Then they can propose alternatives to conventional top-down, "outside-in" approaches.

In this process, we continue to stress that personal relationships are the heartbeat of reform. The conventional

Personal relationships are the heartbeat of reform.

relationships of reform are too often antagonistic: outsiders (including district officials) come in with ideas or programs, without consulting teachers or understanding the school. The resulting conflict is often interpreted as teacher resistance. But with school-initiated reform, teachers are key players in the change design, and conflict is not characterized as resistance but rather as a necessary voice for school improvement. As in previous chapters, *we are impressed with the evidence that reform has taken place most fully in schools that have changed the relationships among adults (and with students) within the school, adopting more collegial and collaborative relationships and more distributed patterns of leadership. These are the personal dimensions of school reform, and only when we get both the personal and the institutional dimensions of reform right will our schools be able to change.*

Focus point

The final section of this chapter reviews the implications of all this for social justice. In particular, if schools cannot change—if we continue to cycle through reforms "again, again, and again"—then it will prove impossible to make schools more equitable places.

A case study that we use throughout this chapter helps to frame our suggestions about the role of teachers in reform. A school we call Franklin Elementary is located in a large urban district and has been in the process of improving its program and services for second-language learners. Prior to the district-initiated reform effort described here, the district had promoted an ESL (English as a second language) framework, based on research-based practices. In collaboration with a nonprofit, countless hours of teacher professional development and support at schools had been devoted to that approach.

However, at the same time the district was pursuing another goal: alignment with a new state framework developed from a state report on English-language development. A new method of teaching language to English-language learners was instituted at Franklin, known by the acronym LEA, for Lenguaje En Acción. It followed a typical pattern of "development," "adoption," "training," "demonstration," "piloting," and "implementation": the district received a state implementation grant, collaborated with a reputable nonprofit in the design, and secured pilot sites. A large binder with readings, model lessons, charts aligning the English-language arts and the new LEA, and benchmark tests accompanied the change. The primary focus of LEA was phonemic understanding. The intent was to allot a full school year for program development, but the project was delayed and could not be implemented at the start of the school year. A novice first-year principal was informed that the school was a pilot site for LEA—something agreed to by the previous principal in order to receive the grant. In the meantime, the new principal had hired an ESL coach; the school was using a balanced literacy framework, based on an extensive investment by the district to pilot and implement a systematic and more balanced literacy approach to the English-language development program. In addition, the teachers were using Guided Language Acquisition Development (GLAD), a more constructivist approach to teaching language that complemented their ESL program and engaged the students in academic talk and vocabulary building, but did not emphasize discrete phonemic skills as the new LEA program did.

Because of the implementation delay, the pilot training started in December, just before winter break. The ESL coach, who learned of the pilot only when the trainers came to talk to the principal in late November, and the teachers reported difficulty seeing the connections between this program and the former framework. Initially, the new program seemed to diminish rather than increase academic talk, contrary to the school's previous focus.

Quite apart from the wisdom of substituting a phonemically based program for a more balanced approach—especially in the middle of the year—this case study highlights several problems inherent in reform and change: top-down initiatives stimulated by a composite of outside authorities (reports, frameworks, nonprofit organizations, funding streams, and the district); the inconsistency of decisions about reform; implementation in schools and teachers without full consultation or understanding of what changes have already taken place; and reversal of years of steady change and professional development, thereby contributing to one form of waste described in Chapter 3. Even though the projects and curricula may have been developed with good intentions, the project was systematically flawed—through no fault of the well-meaning district coordinators, who were persuaded that this initiative would work. District officials replicated bureaucratic, top-down implementation with the unintended consequence of deprofessionalizing teachers—the last thing they would want to think they were doing. As we work through the ways that policy gets developed and formulated, we will see the reasons for such incoherent approaches to reform, and why teachers must play a more active role in change efforts.

COMMISSION REPORTS, FRAMEWORKS, AND STRATEGIC PLANS

The Franklin school case began with alignment objectives that were tied to state frameworks, but it could have just as easily had its genesis in a commission report. *A Nation at Risk* provides a clear example of this peculiarly American genre: although its strident language was partly responsible for its attention (see Tool 5-A), the report summarized a widely accepted view that schooling was central to the country and its international standing. It characterized the American educational system as in need of substantial reform, implicitly critiquing educators for putting our nation at risk. Like a long history of commentary about schooling, the report blamed schools alone for problems arising in other sectors of the economy and in other dimensions of policy (Grubb and Lazerson 2004, ch. 6). Since then, a torrent of reports has issued forth: re-ports on aspects of equity; reports on alternatives to aca-demic competencies (particularly "higher-order skills" or "twenty-first-century skills" like problem-solving and communications); reports emphasizing particular school levels (many focusing on the high school); reports on the use of time, on early childhood programs, on subject-specific reforms like those in math or vocational educa-tion, on the importance of civic education or global edu-cation or environmental education, and on and on. Some commentators have criticized "commissionitis" as a par-ticular disease of the American policy system, but that has not deterred their proliferation.

Reports are useful and instructive to teachers because of the way they analyze problems and make recom-mendations.

Yet the importance of reports should not be ignored. Reports are useful and instructive to teachers because of the way they analyze problems and make recommenda-tions. They start with defining a problem of central im-portance, more important (they claim) than the public has recognized. Commissions focus on their own prob-lem; whether it is the right problem—whether, for exam-ple, the schools were really responsible for the fall in American supremacy before 1983—is never examined. Then, the shift from framing a problem to coming up with recommendations assumes that the report has cor-rectly diagnosed the origin of the problem. The evidence often consists of anecdotal stories about what has gone wrong, or projects that support the recommendations of the report. Because the report is designed to be readable, research-based evidence may either be lacking or rele-gated to obscure working papers. So questions about the nature of evidence need to be raised with commission re-ports, as well as with other reform efforts.

But why should teachers pay attention to commission reports? First, they are instructive as approaches to problem-solving—what not to do! School-level responses to identified problems often mirror commission reports—limited evidence linked to an incomplete analy-sis of the issue, followed by recommendations that may be ill-matched to the actual problem. Second, commission reports are often a hidden factor in decision-making; the recommendations—abbreviated and simplified—often trickle down to districts and then schools. So, if teachers and leaders do not know about reports, they may find themselves indirectly and unknowingly subjected to their recommendations.

A close cousin of the commission report is the policy framework. In addition to recommendations, a framework usually includes readings, surveys, videos, and profiles of schools that have been successful using the framework. Two such frameworks are *Taking Center Stage II* for middle schools, a framework developed by the California Department of Education, and *Breaking Ranks* for middle and high schools, supported by the National Association of Secondary School Principals and Northwest Regional Educational Laboratory. There is nothing particularly wrong with the frameworks these examples lay out. However, with minimal reference to the deep structural issues that confound schools and create inequitable conditions, including the problems with traditional instruction, or of class and race, or of urban conditions, or the powerful tendency of schools to sort students, the frameworks typically do not by themselves result in change. The recommendations usually fail to address these deeper issues because they are all too often the result of many meetings and many voices, and because they have to satisfy multiple constituencies. As a result, they are often bland. For example, this recommendation from *Breaking Ranks* is banal at best: "The school community will promote policies and practices that recognize diversity in accord with the core values of a democratic and civil society and will offer substantive ongoing professional development to help educators appreciate issues of diversity and expose students to a rich array of viewpoints, perspectives, and experiences." "Recognizing diversity" is a pallid recommendation given the depths of racial problems and race-based achievement

gaps in schools, and helping educators "appreciate" diversity is a similarly weak approach given the wide variety of practices available to support students of color. In
addition, it is often easier to pay attention to the framework—for example, to begin the process of aligning existing standards with a framework—than to initiate any
real reforms addressing classroom practice and student
learning. What is particularly disturbing, however, is the
amount of time used to examine frameworks, align them
with current district practices, and raise hopes of leaders
and then teachers. When this happens in succession with
a repeated history of inaction as a result of the framework use, it is extremely difficult to urge teachers to rein-
vest in the next idea that comes down the pike.

However, commission reports and frameworks often
provide a rationale for a reform strategy and have influences of which teachers may be unaware. Take Franklin
Elementary as a case in point. The state Reading and
Language Arts Framework, a 400-page document outlin-
ing grade-level standards and curriculum, offered a foundation for LEA development, as did curriculum
adoption guidelines. These were all available on the Web,
and a diligent teacher could map the framework to the
district, the school, and finally the classroom, but this requires more time than most teachers have. In practice,
then, frameworks often go unnoticed by teachers until it
is too late—until a reform they have not been able to
consider settles upon their school.

A school district's strategic plan usually has more direct impact, with more visible impact on teachers' daily
professional lives. Typically the strategic plan is close on
the heels of a new superintendent, who is hired by the
school board to reform the system. He or she takes time
to assess the district and then engages central office management in writing a "new" strategic plan to make his or
her imprimatur on the district. The plan almost always
asserts that the district is not throwing out the baby with
the bathwater, but it does just that: earlier reforms are

tossed aside, as in the Franklin Elementary case study, and new approaches are developed. All available financial and human resources are marshaled to align school efforts with the "new" strategic plan. The exercise is accompanied by software applications; there are usually glitches in the software, and principals and/or school-based governance teams revise the same old plan in the new form. The entire exercise leads to waste, confusion among teachers, and—because they have had no hand in the new policies—further deprofessionalization and resentment. In urban districts with a series of superintendents, this process is notoriously short-lived, and the result is a series of chaotic messages from the district. Goodwill is squandered again, teachers begin to suffer from "reform fatigue," and the schools still look the same in terms of teaching and learning.

Commission reports, frameworks, and strategic plans are usually developed by policy analysts, business representatives, and state and federal officials who are far from the classroom. Yet teachers and teacher-leaders are in much better positions to understand the possible effects of external plans on schools and classrooms. Teachers then find themselves in impossible situations. A great deal of time is required to keep up with external documents. When they engage with outside experts or question parts of the implementation, teachers are often viewed as resisters rather than partners with the district office. Though multiple unintended consequences of policy or program implementation could be avoided by engaging teachers in the development, this is rare. Finally, because of the hierarchical nature of districts and planning processes, reports and plans are often printed for distribution and posted on websites before there is opportunity for teacher comment—as was the case in the Franklin Elementary reform, coming from the outside into the school without much warning. So even as we advocate for more teacher understanding of the thrust and resulting influence of commission reports and reform frameworks, it may be more productive to consider completely different approaches to reform.

TAKING CHARGE OF REFORM

A strong alternative—or perhaps a complement—to top-down and outside-in reform engages teachers and leaders in changes initiated and implemented at the *school* level. These approaches build upon and reinforce the autonomy and professionalism of teachers, rather than de-professionalizing them. Because they emerge from the concerns of a particular school, they are more likely to be adjusted to the needs of students within that school and can build on the history of the school. We summarize key reform voices who have called for this approach. We then highlight some of the evidence in favor of school-initiated reform before discussing briefly what complementary or "hybrid" approaches might be.

In his well-known critique of reform efforts, "Reforming Again, Again, and Again," Larry Cuban (1990) describes three types of reforms—*instructional, curricular,* and *governance.* Public institutions engage in reform because they respond to public opinion and the push for innovation to solve problems—many of which, especially in education, lie outside the sphere that schools could ever expect to influence. They do this by trying novel programs, joining regional and national efforts to improve curriculum, and adopting innovative technologies that satisfy the public demand to improve schools. The local implementation of ideas that come from elsewhere is typically not well supervised, however, and thus the overall reform effort is only loosely connected to what happens in the classroom because teachers continue to make pedagogical and curricular decisions. Teachers question changes when reforms (or even mandates) do not fit their belief systems about teaching and learning—just as the teachers in Franklin Elementary resisted a new curriculum based more on phonemic awareness than on balanced practices. Reforms recur because the underlying problems persist and pressure remains to do something, despite solutions poorly matched to the underlying problems; countless hours of goodwill and energy are expended for limited outcomes. Worse than going nowhere, the reform efforts with little impact tend to compromise the next effort because the teachers are more hesitant to commit themselves. Teacher autonomy tends to carry the day, as they are the ones in classrooms actually teaching; the result is fragmented implementation with limited shared responsibility for outcomes.

Another longtime observer of reform, Richard Elmore (2004), distinguishes three levels of school cohesion: the atomized school, the school with emerging cohesion, and the cohesive school. The *atomized* school is the traditional school, in which the egg carton analogy is apt. Teachers, individually responsible for student outcomes, have few structures for teacher collaboration, and the traditional hierarchical model of leadership prevails. The school with *emerging cohesion* includes more shared expectations and developing internal accountability, led by a principal with vision and an eye for collective leadership.

In the *fully cohesive and collaborative* school, because of its internal structures, the school is poised to respond to outside demands for change or accountability. It is able to muster its members to question, provide data, and decide if the reform is appropriate, and if it decides to push back it does so from a position of knowledge and authority. When external accountability mechanisms are inevitable, it can leverage other forms of accountability to provide a more comprehensive picture of student learning. In the case of Franklin Elementary, for example, cohesion at the school was emerging. But the circumstances of a new principal, a new ESL coach, and a persuasive push from trusted district colleagues resulted in implementation before teachers could learn about it or decide whether they thought it was a good idea, in effect sidetracking their internal development.

In addition to Elmore's three stages we add a fourth: the *pre-atomized* school. The difference in this school is that teacher accountability and professionalism are undeveloped, the school is disorganized, there is no leadership (either hierarchical or distributed), and the response to external demands is often chaotic and superficial; the principal often has a reactive stance to external authority and projects any problems onto the teaching staff—who in turn blame students for problems. Many pre-atomized schools lack even the minimal cohesion of the atomized or traditional school. In this situation it may be tempting for districts to bring in a "strong" principal—that is, an authoritarian principal—to restore order. But that tactic can only lengthen the time needed to become an internally cohesive school, and given the history of a school, it may remain atomized for a long period of time.

Michael Fullan (2007) also provides clear lessons for teachers rethinking their participation in reform and change. Three of his maxims of change are consistent with different roles for teachers and with the necessity of different personal relations within cohesive schools: (1) *Problems are our friends.* Because school culture is highly dependent on getting along personally as well as professionally, teachers do not always view dissent and conflict as positive—in each other and their students. To the contrary, "Conflict is not just a nuisance: it is positively necessary in working out new productive solutions" (Fullan 2007, 15). A central difference in the cohesive school is that conflict is not personal; it is based on differences of opinion (hopefully well informed and evidence based) of what to do, and the resulting discussions proceed not by attacking people but by expressing different opinions about their ideas. The need for depersonalized debate harks back to a key purpose of schools—the preparation of citizens and the practice of democracy; like schooling itself, it may be messy and complex, but common purpose and direction can be achieved only through dialogue. (2) *Practice fearlessness.* Hierarchical organizations are dependent on rule-followers, and

Conflict is not just a nuisance: it is positively necessary in working out new productive solutions.

many teachers in conventional schools feel more comfortable placating and/or avoiding conflict. But Fullan reminds us that collective change relies on a sense of courage to embrace creativity and possibility. Of course, this attribute intersects with the teacher-leaders as social justice advocates, who do not simply accept outside choices for them or their school. The discussion at the end of the chapter describes effective approaches to conflict and difference. (3) *Give up the search for the silver bullet;* there is no one right answer. Rather, teacher-leaders use school-based evidence and appropriate research to craft the reform agenda and build theories of change, testing them against new situations. They view each day as an experiment—the heart and soul of their professional development and identity.

Roland Barth (1990, 2003, 2007) has repeated the same basic mantra in writing about school change. Reform happens best from *within*, not from without, a basic premise of this entire book, and is based on teachers' analyses of their situation (see Tool 5-B). "Unless adults talk with one another, observe one another, and help one another, very little will change" (Barth 1990, 32). We must presume that teachers have the disposition and ability to be critical friends to each other as colleagues, as we discussed in Chapter 2. Of course, it makes sense that teachers learn from other teachers, and professional development should be generated from their issues and suggestions. Yet, internal forms of professional development do require some governance structure, particularly a leadership team that can make appropriate decisions about professional development and, based on evidence about internal expertise, decide when to engage outside expertise for the benefit of the change.

School people must confront the cautious, resistant, fearful "other" that resides within each of us before confronting others who are without.

In conventional schools, the all-important ability to trust is compromised by the way outside policies and district mandates press down on schools and teachers: districts and states are continually judging schools and teachers and blaming them for failures in student performance. In turn this leads teachers to externalize blame, to focus on the district or parents or colleagues as responsible for poor school performance. Then, teacher talk about school issues follows a pattern that Eugene Eubanks, Ralph Parish, and Dianne Smith (1997) call "Discourse I," which is unproductive conversation generally characterized by blaming others, seeking magic solutions where none exist (contrary to Fullan's maxim), focusing only on marginal improvements ("tinkering"), taking the (ineffective) advice of outside experts unfamiliar with the school, and relying on technical methods (like a district planning process) to drive change. Discourse I is more familiar in top-down, outside-in reforms, which by nature limit how teachers talk about change and reform.

The alternative to Discourse I is the school-based model of change. Rather than seeking magic bullets, this approach considers an issue from many sides with several possible solutions. It converts the antagonist language of Discourse I, "us versus them," to "we" by making deep changes in the way adults within a school take collective responsibility for outcomes. It admits that reform and change are messy and complex, sometimes ambiguous, and often experimental ("what could we do differently?") and does not resort to blaming language ("it doesn't work; I told you so"). Conversations within Discourse II, with fundamentally different assumptions about the change process, can become the daily professional work of teachers and leaders, developing the kind of school culture that promotes more effective adult and student learning.

From these perspectives the top-down, outside-in approach to school reform is not the best avenue to innovation and lasting change. Bottom-up and inside-out approaches have been well represented by those who have analyzed the process of change over the past few decades (or indeed, over the entire history of public schools, as Cuban has). We are impressed with the empirical evidence supporting school-based change. Many of the accounts of exemplary schools describe schools (or sometimes individual departments) that have restructured themselves as professional learning communities, with extensive collaboration among teachers about developing curricula, examining students' work, and formulating their own conceptions of curriculum and pedagogy—like the two math departments described by Rochelle Gutierrez (2000) and Jo Boaler and Megan Staples (2008). Many of the exemplary teachers and classrooms described in Mike Rose's *Possible Lives* exist in more democratic schools. The schools with internal accountability described in *The New Accountability* (Carnoy, Elmore, and Siskin 2003) have similarly developed relations of trust and reciprocal accountability among the adults in those schools, and these turn out to be preconditions for meeting the requirements of external accountability. And the conceptions of resources articulated in Chapter 3 clarify that many of the most effective resources in schools are collective, and that they must be constructed by teachers and leaders working collaboratively. We're far from having "proof," whatever that might be, but substantial evidence indicates that trusting relationships among adults are the fundamental prerequisites for any school change and for the institutional improvements that constitute real reform.

There is, to be sure, an intermediate position, because school-level change does not and cannot occur in a vacuum. A balanced approach to school reform exists, with districts and schools collaborating in designing and implementing reforms—what Tyack and Cuban (1995, ch. 6) call a "hybridized" approach. Some of the apparently exemplary districts profiled in Chapter 4 have also managed to developed a "distributed" approach to reform, in which districts collaborate with schools about reforms and assess the readiness of each school for reform, rather than assuming that a single reform fits all schools, the dreaded pattern of "one size fits all."

However, a caution about maintaining a balance in these hybrid approaches is necessary: most reforms come into schools the same way—from the project to the district to the school, not from inside the school to the district. Thus, the choice of implementation sites is district-driven, sometimes with good intentions of spreading resources to low-performing schools, but then they either have to be "sold" to schools or mandated for implementation; in some cases, the district has written a grant with particular sites in mind. In the case of Franklin Elementary, the former principal agreed to it as a site for implementation, but without teacher discussion or agreement. The school lacked any internal decision-making processes to decide what projects to adopt. In the end the staff were unable to modify the district's plan in any way. Though a "balanced" approach to reform seems the best way to combine district resources and support with school-level initiative and participation, such a balance requires that both the district and the school have the appropriate mechanisms of deliberation and planning in place. So there's no substitute for schools developing internal accountability, cohesion, and distributed decision-making structures. Only then can teachers and leaders make sure that district initiatives, even nominally "balanced" ones, are fully integrated into schools.

There's no substitute for schools developing internal accountability, cohesion, and distributed decision-making structures.

REASONABLE, RATIONAL APPROACHES TO REFORM

No matter who initiates or "owns" a reform, changes should be based on some conception or theory of change, explaining why a particular reform is appropriate to the problem being addressed, and why it will generate desirable outcomes. Otherwise, reforms are likely to be based on casual theories and evidence, or imitation of what other districts are doing, or other poorly justified approaches. Although there are several theories of change, there is no one conception that completely fits any given situation or school. So again, a hybrid or balanced approach derived from all these theories may assist schools in paying attention to the multiple factors that any change process entails, and it may help maintain flexibility. The three approaches to change that we highlight are *technical-rational, short cycles of inquiry,* and *sightings.* Each of the change theories has upsides and downsides. All of these theories of change support collecting and analyzing systematic evidence, which we discuss in the following section of this chapter.

Key concept
technical-rational
theory of change

A **technical-rational theory of change** presumes that schools are rational organizations and they operate the best when there is a long-range plan tightly connected to clear and measurable outcomes—like an annual strategic plan. The technical-rational approach is closely related to the techniques of policy analysis in the policy-making world. This approach, as well as the less rigid cycle of inquiry, usually starts by defining a problem, or goals and objectives, or measurable outcomes. This often proves to be one of the most difficult stages, because there may be disagreement about which of several different formulations of a problem will lead to lasting change. The approach should be based on a cogent *theory of action* and a clear conception of how the action plan will result in addressing the problem and achieving the goals (as we defined the term in Chapter 4). Implementation is based on consistency of action; without clarity and consistency, various implementation problems arise. A plan should allow for midcourse corrections. If participants are too tightly committed to the original plan, there is no opportunity to draw on unexpected results or ideas that arise during the process.

Key concept
cycle of
inquiry (COI)

The short **cycle of inquiry (COI)** is based on the understanding that schools are not as rational as we would like. The COI has more room for adjustment because longer-term planning is likely to go awry (Fullan 1997). Michael Schmoker's (1999) approach to short cycles has been helpful to schools. This approach recognizes that institutions are not completely rational organizations with tight relationships between means and ends. Initially a plan calls for short "wins" to gain momentum for a change and frequent reflection about the process and products of change. These recursive cycles of inquiry rely on collaborative structures within schools to develop and implement plans, rather than a centralized implementation plan to which all participants must be faithful. COIs are therefore more congruent with the collective school than is the model of technical-rational change, though both use problem formulation, identification of solutions, and implementation of these solutions to achieve their goals.

The approach based on "sightings" is somewhat different. **Sightings** are anomalous and interesting events that occur during the change process and provide deeper understanding of a school, its students, the teachers and leaders in the school, or direction (McDonald 1996). Using sightings to promote change relies in part on the sudden realization ("aha!") of how to address an issue; that realization is triggered by the intersection of intuition and experience (Dewey 1938). The sighting can be used as momentum to move forward—or conversely, to question an outside intervention. In the Franklin Elementary case, for example, teachers knew experientially that many parts of the new curriculum did not match their knowledge, experience, or school direction. Sightings therefore provide motivation to a school community, but more important, they can be potent actions for developing a more creative solution. The power of sightings relies on the strength of evidence generated inside the school; even more than cycles of inquiry, they arise from and are embedded in the trusting relationships within a school. Of course, there is a downside to reliance on sightings without planning; the result can be incoherence. That leads to disjointed progress and undermines reform efforts.

Key concept
sightings

These three approaches provide guidelines for school change when that change is initiated from inside or outside the school. They can help teachers inside schools understand what outside experts use as their theory of change when designing and implementing reforms. All three approaches require participants to think about the theories of action underlying change, the rate of change, the readiness of the participants, and the support necessary to make sure that the change effort is clear, consistent, and self-generating. They also require a deeper look at underlying causes of the problem before planning solutions. Peter Senge's "Five Whys" is a relatively straightforward exercise that helps a school community ferret out these causes (see Tool 5-C).

There are always pros and cons for any theory of change. A balanced approach might incorporate elements from all three and might include the problem formulation and search for solutions of the technical-rational approach, the flexibility of the logic of inquiry, a lookout for sightings of unusual interest, and the regular collection and use of evidence to make sure the change process has not gone awry.

At the Franklin school, the LEA project had many characteristics of a technical-rational approach and fewer characteristics of short cycles of inquiry or sightings. There were limited attempts to contextualize; certainly there was no meeting with the ESL coach or principal or teacher-leaders to sufficiently assess their school or enable them to offer alternatives. The training was not customized. Although the term *pilot project* implies that this kind of adjustment should take place as the project is implemented, the teachers experienced the implementation as more rigid, with rules and formulas about how to carry out lessons. Furthermore, it was not obvious to teachers how evidence from each session might be used to inform the direction or to make changes. Even though it was based on a rational conception of change, the LEA plan did not take account of the history of the school and the inconsistencies between the new and former processes for teaching second-language learners. Without a more balanced approach to change, the project had limited possibility for achieving the outcomes it sought.

EVIDENCE-BASED PRACTICE

The three models of change presented in the prior section all require evidence—to understand when a problem is serious enough to address, to understand the potential causes of a problem, to document the changes (or lack of changes) in response to an initiative, and to evaluate more formally whether a reform has worked. When schools want to invest in effective resources, as we argued in Chapter 3, it's necessary to understand "what works." Yet when we suggest to aspiring principals that decisions should be based on evidence and data, we are fully aware that impressions about the school substitute as "evidence." Lunchroom talk and hallway gossip, anecdotes rather than evidence, often direct improvement. The basic difference between anecdote and evidence is how systematic the information is, how it is collected, how reliable and valid the data-collection instruments are, and how people in schools use evidence to inform change. Improving the quality and use of evidence is critical if teachers and leaders are to develop their own information in verifying learning and making instructional and organizational decisions. Without such evidence, the king of all data—standardized test scores—becomes the sole measure of achievement and reform, and teachers and schools cede control of change to outsiders.

Instead, teachers can broaden their knowledge of what counts as evidence of student achievement and other outcomes, but they can do that only if they fully understand multiple measures of student progress and various forms of evidence. What counts as "evidence" has been furiously debated, especially since No Child Left Behind. The presumed "gold standard" of evidence, according to the Bush-era Institute for Educational Science, has been information from random-assignment studies, even though these can be used only for carefully defined programs and are unethical in many cases. The What Works Clearinghouse established by the federal

government has similarly used a narrow conception of
evidence, including only studies based on random assignment or sophisticated statistical techniques, and ex-
cluding all qualitative research. This information is
difficult for individuals other than researchers to understand, and indeed reports generated by the clearinghouse
are written in language that makes then inaccessible to
principals and teachers. Another type of evidence comes
from systematic reviews of the existing research, including both qualitative and quantitative studies, often ap-
pearing in the *Review of Educational Research* or the new
Journal of Research on Educational Effectiveness, or in
publications from think tanks like the RAND Corporation. Certainly the Web gives teachers access to this kind
of evidence, which could inform their ideas.

But neither of these sources includes much evidence
from the classroom and the school. The evidence generated by teacher-leaders and administrators as the basis for
internal reform efforts takes many forms. One form, focusing on student learning, includes the kinds of teacher-
developed assessments reviewed in Chapter 2. These can
range from formative assessments (taking place minute
to minute in the classroom and including quizzes, unit
tests, and performance tasks at designated times in the
yearly schedule) to summative assessments (paper-and-
pencil benchmark, projects, exhibitions, portfolios) and
finally to criterion-referenced standardized tests. Teachers
need to find or develop assessments that are more authentic tasks and that provide evidence of student learning, including multiple measures of learning, because
standardized tests, given once a year, are inadequate and
incomplete measures of learning. In a collective school,
once teachers have reshaped their instruction to include
daily, weekly, and quarterly assessments, they need to examine the student data and student work together to
make certain they agree on what high-quality work looks
like.

Another widely used type of evidence is the survey,
which often gauges teacher and student perceptions

about a variety of subjects under the umbrella of school culture and climate. Unlike the anecdote and hallway talk, surveys attempt to collect information from a wide range of teachers or students, not just those who happen to talk the loudest (as the school in Chapter 2 did) to gain a more complete picture of what all faculty were thinking about an issue. To be sure, sometimes surveys are poorly constructed, though there are sources of help from educational laboratories or reputable school reform organizations, with instruments that have been used and refined with large numbers of respondents. Other surveys that might serve the needs of schools can be found on the Web (e.g., at www.nsrf.org).

A useful alternative to surveys is the fishbowl process, or focus group. A predetermined set of questions (perhaps devised by a school's leadership team) is forwarded to the entire group. A recorder (or two) keeps accurate notes that serve as evidence. A subset of persons is asked to begin the fishbowl process: Six to eight people form a circle with one empty chair placed in the middle; any observer can enter the conversation by sitting on the empty chair. The original six to eight people may move in and out of the circle, providing space for others to enter. The facilitator is critical for keeping the process focused on the original questions. This kind of structured process offers a forum for more voices and a mechanism for collecting evidence from a wider range of participants. The process can be transposed to classrooms to collect feedback from students.

Four types of classroom-level evidence are lesson logs on formative assessments, grade books, student work, and peer observations. For example, a group of four third-grade teachers improved instruction of writing by using the following sequence: (1) scanning four lesson plans from each teacher to get a general sense of the form and flow; (2) highlighting the elements that stood out to other teachers; (3) noting the relationship of the lesson objective to any assessments in the lesson plan; (4) collecting the themes that emerged from this process, which in this specific case included similarities among teachers, differences, and puzzling features; (5) listing two to three items under each of the three themes; (6) talking with partners; and (7) changing their lesson plans to be more consistent across the grade level. During the next week, each teacher used the revised lesson plan with similar assessments, conducted an observation of one other teacher using a common protocol, and analyzed his or her observation notes with a similar process. This was followed by looking at student writing work with the same care and attention to detail.

These procedures correspond to what Judith Warren Little (1982) recommended long ago. Teachers must talk to each other about issues of practice and should observe one another; they should focus together on curriculum; and they can teach each other. In short, to be authentic colleagues they must learn from their work together. These practices include all teachers, focus on teaching and learning, give teachers control over their own work, support an effective kind of internal professional development, and engage teachers intellectually. The evidence collected includes the results of classroom observations with revised lesson plans; with enough teachers participating, this may summarize the efforts of teachers over weeks or even months of change.

No matter how data are collected, teachers and administrators often neglect their analysis. A person or small group needs to extract a few themes or conclusions from the evidence to use as the basis for next steps. Becoming proficient at determining patterns and themes and regrouping responses according to "big ideas" or themes help immensely in the school reform process, because teachers can then understand the evidence they have collected and appreciate its value for the changes the school makes.

In the touchstone case of Franklin Elementary, much of the evidence necessary to inform classroom practice was lacking. Tests for phonemic development were administered periodically, but the sample lesson plans included no provisions to link the objectives to assessments, and they failed to demonstrate how a teacher might know if the students achieved the daily objectives. The weekly planning guides listed the content and skills desired and what the teacher should do, but they neglected all evidence about student learning and therefore provided little information either to guide the next session or to judge the success of the pilot. In the end, the lack of teacher-generated evidence meant that the pilot project generated almost no information about the usefulness of this approach in the future.

Overall, then, teachers need to consider a broad range of evidence when designing and implementing reforms. But they should not think of evidence only as published research carried out by professors in faraway universities and think tanks. Indeed, that kind of evidence is often seriously incomplete because it cannot do what teacher research and school-based evidence can do—understand the particularities of a school, its history, its students, its teachers, and other resources. Only by drawing on a variety of evidence can we begin to understand which reforms might improve our schools for all students. Reasserting the teachers' role in collecting, analyzing, and using evidence to inform change efforts is another way to become agents of reform in our schools.

SOCIAL JUSTICE AND SCHOOL REFORM

The way educators approach reform provides an important signal of their commitment to social justice and equity as the province of teachers, not outsiders. A top-down, outside-in approach signals that central policymakers, with their analysts and promoters, are in control of schools, and that principals and teachers are important only in obeying reform plans faithfully. This is a didactic approach to reform, with a hierarchical and behaviorist pedagogy embedded in it (Cohen and Ball 1993)—just as the teacher as lecturer and source of all knowledge creates a hierarchy and behaviorist relationships in the classroom. The alternative—the bottom-up, teacher-generated and -facilitated approach, with teachers gathering and working collaboratively with leaders to analyze evidence—sends a different message about relations in a school: that all participants are necessary to make the collective school work well. Then teachers and leaders, more aware of how commission reports, policy frameworks, and district change work, can use that understanding to chart a different and more productive reform narrative. Teachers who develop skills in understanding and then managing change and reform can better respond when a district decides, for example, that their school will be a pilot site for a project or a full-school reform.

The driving reason for developing a different narrative about reform is that the old one has worked poorly. Whether it is Larry Cuban's historical analysis of "reforming again, again, and again," the sequential stages of reform since 1983, the frequency with which one reform is displaced by another, or the story of schools like Franklin Elementary School and its conflicting reforms, they all signal a need for an alternative approach. The outside-in approach—with problems and their solutions formulated outside schools, unaware of what resources (in the broad sense of Chapter 3) are necessary to enact reform—is simply ineffective. In addition, if schools are inequitable—if they provide different levels of the resources that matter to different groups of students, marked by their race and ethnicity, their language, their family conditions, the attitudes they have about schools and teachers, and what they mean—then the inability to reform implies the inability to correct these inequities. *We can never have equitable schools unless we can change the schools we now have, and we cannot reform our schools without teachers, teacher-leaders, and the administrators who work with them assuming collective responsibility for their work and student outcomes.*

Focus point

DISCUSSION QUESTIONS

1. What is the history of reform efforts in your school? Drawing on the historical memory or interviews with veteran teachers, past principals, or central office personnel, reconstruct the reform and change history at the school by making a timeline of reform and professional development. (NOTE: Do not think of only the big projects, but also projects that might have involved teachers who demonstrated success or professional growth). You could make a rubric for how successful the reform or project was or is and then list the attributes that made for success.

2. Look at two or three recent efforts and analyze what theory of change was most at work in each reform effort. Decide how the reform effort was mostly from outside, mostly from inside, or a hybrid version. What about the change process worked or did not work?

3. Map the current reforms at your school in terms of origin, theory of action (espoused or in action), persons involved, evidence, and results.

4. What daily evidence do you collect in your classroom? How do you share evidence to support change in classroom practice?

FURTHER READING

Barth, Roland. 1990. *Improving Schools from Within: Teachers, Parents, and Principals Can Make a Difference.* San Francisco: Jossey-Bass.

Cuban, Larry. 1990. "Reforming Again, Again, and Again." *Educational Researcher* 19, 3: 3–13.

Elmore, Richard. 2004. "When Accountability Knocks." In *School Reform from the Inside Out.* Cambridge, MA: Harvard Education Press.

Eubanks, Eugene, Ralph Parish, and Dianne Smith. 1997. "Changing the Discourse in Schools." In Peter Hall, ed., *Race, Ethnicity, and Multicultural Policy and Practice.* New York: Garland Publishing.

Fullan, Michael. 2007. *The NEW Meaning of Educational Change.* New York: Teachers College Press.

Karp, Stan. 2003. "Drive-by School Reform." In L. Christensen and S. Karp, eds., *Rethinking School Reform: Views from the Classroom*. Milwaukee, WI: Rethinking Schools, Ltd.

Tyack, David, and Larry Cuban. 1995. *Tinkering Toward Utopia: A Century of Public School Reform*. Cambridge, MA: Harvard University Press.

TOOL 5-A: TEACHER DISCUSSION OF COMMISSION REPORTS

This exercise can be repeated with a more recent commission report relevant to your school, rather than *A Nation at Risk*.

- Examine the language in the excerpt. Much like the call to action after the USSR launch of Sputnik in 1957, this document had a powerful effect on education reform because of its language. What generalizations can you draw?
- What, according to the chapter, were the results of this publication?
- Why is historical context important for teachers undertaking reform?

A Nation at Risk

Our Nation is at risk. Our once unchallenged preeminence in commerce, industry, science, and technological innovation is being overtaken by competitors throughout the world. This report is concerned with only one of the many causes and dimensions of the problem, but it is the one that undergirds American prosperity, security, and civility. We report to the American people that while we can take justifiable pride in what our schools and colleges have historically accomplished and contributed to the United States and the well-being of its people, the educational foundations of our society are presently being eroded by a rising tide of mediocrity that threatens our very future as a Nation and a people. What was unimaginable a generation ago has begun to occur—others are matching and surpassing our educational attainments.

If an unfriendly foreign power had attempted to impose on America the mediocre educational performance that exists today, we might well have viewed it as an act of war. As it stands, we have allowed this to happen to ourselves. We have even squandered the gains in student achievement made in the wake of the Sputnik challenge. Moreover, we have dismantled essential support systems which helped make those gains possible. We have, in effect, been committing an act of unthinking, unilateral educational disarmament.

Our society and its educational institutions seem to have lost sight of the basic purposes of schooling, and of the high expectations and disciplined effort needed to attain them. This report, the result of 18 months of study, seeks to generate reform of our educational system in fundamental ways and to renew the Nation's commitment to schools and colleges of high quality throughout the length and breadth of our land. (Available at http://www.ed.gov/pubs/NatAtRisk/risk.html)

TOOL 5-B: ROLAND BARTH'S CONCEPTION OF CHANGE

- Read this statement first silently as teachers highlight or underline the most compelling words or phrases.
- Next, have a "popcorn" read-out—directing participants to speak as the spirit moves them. Repetition is fine.
- Thinking about the fruitfulness of interactions at your school and then imagining your school as a fruit, which one would you choose and why?

If the critical school issues like evaluation and placement are ever to become fruitful occasions that bring teacher and principal together in the service of students and the school—that is, if the capacity of teachers and principals to enrich rather than diminish each other's lives and work is to be realized, conditions must change. Somehow the school principal must assume more of the burden of protecting the best interests of teachers and liberating more of the constructive power of which teachers are capable. In addition each teacher will have to assume more ownership for the best interests of the school—including other teachers, other teachers' pupils, and the principal. A key to improving schools from within, then, lies in improving the interactions among teachers and between teachers and principals. (Barth 1990, p. 28)

TOOL 5-C: THE FIVE WHYS: GETTING TO THE UNDERLYING ISSUE

"The Five Whys" is suggested by Peter Senge (1990) as a tool to help articulate difficult problems and to uncover their systemic causes. Experience has shown that it is important to fully understand the problem at its deepest level in order to identify the strategy or direction that will be the most effective. Experience has also shown that many change efforts neglect this crucial problem identification and problem-posing step.

The Activity

1. Formulate a problem statement around a core issue, perhaps choosing from several that are proposed.

2. Ask why that problem exists, and brainstorm many possible answers. Then label those responses as IN our sphere of influence to change or OUT of our sphere of influence to change.

3. Choose *one* of the answers from the IN list to brainstorm further, and ask "why" regarding this statement, *going deeper on one issue.*

4. Brainstorm many possible answers to this new "why" question, *going deeper on that question* (reminder—choose an IN our sphere of influence to change at each level).

5. Repeat the process five times, or as many times as are necessary to go deep, until the group has arrived at core, systemic issues/ roots or underlying causes.

6. Debrief the activity to learn from the process. Be explicit about the group's learning from this experience.

Important Notes on the Process

- Begin with an important, authentic problem—not an event.
- Avoid blaming individuals.
- Avoid answering the question by focusing on specific events.

- Use why as a symptom to go deeper to the underlying cause or root cause or structural issue.
- Resist the temptation to solve the problem. Focus on inquiry instead.

The facilitator might ask some questions during the activity to help the process:

Are these issues going to take us deeper in our understanding?
What are the issues that we can do something about?
Where could we look for evidence of this problem?

CHAPTER SIX

ACHIEVING SOCIAL JUSTICE AND EQUITY

I N AN INEQUITABLE SOCIETY, a central challenge for public schools is that they are responsible for enhancing equity even as inequalities seep into schools in so many ways. It's no wonder, then, that developing more equitable schools sometimes seems overwhelming. There is no easy solution to this problem, but if teachers and school leaders were consistent participants in promoting equity—in all their roles, as teachers and leaders and citizens and members of unions and professional associations—then surely progress would be possible.

In this chapter we summarize many of the points about equity made earlier in the book, in the first section on achieving *distributive justice*. **Distributive justice** refers to the distribution of valuable aspects of education, whether that refers to access to educational opportunities, to money and spending, to effective resources like those we examined in Chapter 3, or to educational outcomes. Distributive justice sometimes requires actions at the classroom level, and sometimes at the school level. Often, higher levels of government or district policy are necessary, recapitulating the results from Chapters 4 and 5. Unions and professional associations can participate in the intellectual and political battles over equitable education. And

Key concept
distributive justice

everyone joins in defining what schools are supposed to be, in our roles as citizens and taxpayers, as parents and community members. Some teachers will choose to work exclusively in the classroom; others will become union activists or participants in district or state politics. But everyone can benefit from understanding the different environments in which efforts to achieve equity take place.

However, distributive justice is usually a *static* concept—it looks at what resources different students have at particular points in time, or what outcomes can be measured at certain crucial moments (like fourth grade, or the end of high school). What really counts for individual students is *dynamic* inequality—the differences among students that develop over many years of schooling. Unfortunately, our schools are not structured to worry much about dynamic inequality, and certainly the data we collect about students are usually static or cross-sectional data—data on test scores at specific grade levels, for example, rather than measures of learning that track a student's development over time. Shifting from a static to a dynamic concept of equity is therefore difficult and unfamiliar, even though it describes much more accurately how inequality develops—and therefore what educators must do to prevent inequalities from becoming worse over time. The second section of this chapter therefore examines what we can learn by taking an explicitly dynamic approach to equity.

**Key concept
dynamic
inequality**

(In contrast to the static conceptions of distributive justice, **dynamic inequality** is concern with the differences among students that develop over the many years of schooling, from kindergarten to twelfth grade and beyond.)

**Key concept
procedural
justice**

Distributive justice (whether static or dynamic) is concerned with the distribution of valued resources, with who gets what. A different concept of justice involves **procedural justice**, the justice or injustice inherent in the processes or procedures used in schools—or, outside of schools, in the court system, in the policing mechanisms in our communities, or in the tax system. Students' sense of fairness in schools, or their feelings of being wronged, often come from violations of procedural justice. The most pervasive examples involve discipline; however, as with distributive justice, there are many other kinds of procedural justice, including treatment by teachers, selection procedures for low-status tracks like special education or high-status tracks like Advanced Placement (AP) classes, and decisions about student rights. Violations of procedural justice can be countered by various reforms, especially revisions of unfair procedures. In addition, reformers sometimes propose democratic schools, in which students play greater roles in decisions about discipline, conflict resolutions, and school governance. Even if such fundamental changes in how schools operate are rare, knowing about the landscape of procedural justice may alert teachers and leaders to dimensions of justice in schools, and possibilities for enhancing justice, that they might otherwise miss.

(Procedural justice refers not to the distribution of valued aspects of schooling, but to the justice of the procedures used in schools, for example, to discipline students or to choose students for particular programs or tracks.)

Finally, we have stressed throughout this book that there are some inequalities in schools that come from the larger inequalities in society: inequality in earnings (described in Tool 1-B); in other dimensions of family background, such as parental education and occupational influences; in health care; in housing; and in the neighborhood conditions conducive to stable family life. It has sometimes been difficult for educators to articulate the need for these noneducational policies, because when they do so they have been accused of blaming schooling outcomes on *families*, rather than recognizing what *schools* could do better. But what we need in this country is a *both/and* policy—*both* improvements in education *and* improvements in those noneducational policies that support education—rather than the *either/or* approaches we often see, particularly when policymakers try to turn social problems into educational problems. The fourth section of this chapter therefore raises the question of which noneducational policies might be necessary to achieve equity, as well as which educational reforms.

The social justice agenda is enormous and daunting. This is the inevitable consequence of making schools responsible for correcting inequality in a country with relatively high levels of inequality. But this is a good moment in our history for educators to think about the multiple dimension of inequality partly since a new administration headed by Barack Obama has signaled its support for a more activist government, and partly because the financial crisis since 2008 has clarified how wrong free-market rhetoric is.

SUMMARIZING DISTRIBUTIVE JUSTICE IN SCHOOLS

Throughout this book, we have raised a number of issues of distributive justice; that is, how different aspects of education are distributed. To determine whether certain educational practices and outcomes are just or equitable, however, it's first necessary to have a conception of equity. Readers of this book might first think about what their own conceptions of equity are, and what they think equality of educational opportunity—a particularly slippery concept—is. Tool 6-A clarifies that there have been many historical conceptions of equity in this country, ranging from the most basic—for example, eliminating the barriers that once prohibited African American students and women from entering certain schools—to compensatory conceptions in which those with greater educational needs are provided more resources rather than less. These can be applied to access to schooling, the most basic dimension; to money and spending per student, the subject of so many lawsuits and legislative battles; to resources, in the broad conceptions of resources we developed in Chapter 3; or to outcomes like learning and test scores, high school graduation rates, or access to

college. The result of different conceptions of equity applied to different dimensions of schooling is a large map
or "landscape" of equity. These have been applied in different ways to various practices, reforms, and lawsuits in
education, as Tool 6-A clarifies with examples of different
conceptions of equity. One implication is that we don't
all agree what equity is; for example, those who believe
that equity requires equal funding disagree with those
pressing for equal outcomes, and those who believe fairness demands equal treatment of all students (including
"color blindness") disagree with those who argue that equity requires allocating more resources to low-performing
students (or to racially specific policies).

The responsibility for ensuring distributive justice rests
with many different people, at different levels of the education system. In many ways, distributive justice starts in
the classroom. The central responsibility of teachers is to
be able to teach effectively. As was discussed in Chapters
1 and 3, mastering a range of teaching approaches—
including more constructivist or "balanced" or innovative approaches—is essential. That requires general pedagogical knowledge and pedagogical content knowledge,
as well as content knowledge or mastery of the subject
one is teaching, together with practice and guidance to
be able to use this knowledge in the classroom. These
and other dimensions of instructional practice are resources, as we reviewed in Chapter 3, even though they
cannot be simply bought. Although individual teachers
may develop innovative approaches to teaching on their
own, by trial and error or imitation of other strong
teachers, we think it more likely that effective instructional practices emerge when a *school* develops them
among all its teachers, and when teacher-leaders and
principals act as instructional leaders. Conversely, failing
to address instructional approaches consistently, and allowing accountability and standard tests to drive curriculum and instruction, ensure that schools will remain
unequal in both instructional resources and outcomes.

In addition, a crucial resource in every school is the way teachers treat students, an observation virtually everyone makes and often embodied in the slogan that "teaching is all about relationships." However, the supportive treatment of students is itself a resource that may be unequally distributed, as some teachers—"warm demanders"—develop supportive relationships with students whereas others are brusque, authoritarian, or simply indifferent. In some schools, the treatment of students varies by race and ethnicity, by family background or class, and sometimes by gender and other student characteristics—the many forms of mistreatment we explored in Chapter 3. There are methods for overcoming these inequalities in treatment, and some teachers may adopt them on their own. But overcoming patterns of mistreatment is better treated as a *school* issue, within a school with collaborative and trusting relationships. In such a setting, courageous conversations about race and class can often clarify the dilemmas of unequal learning, classroom observations can identify patterns in the treatment of different children, and sustained professional development can help teachers learn the methods proposed in culturally relevant pedagogy and multicultural education. Supportive treatment of students is a responsibility of every teacher, but there are collective and institutional aspects of these crucial resources as well.

The quality of instruction is certainly unequally distributed, but in Chapter 3 we argued that a great variety of school resources affect learning and progress through schooling—certainly the complex resources involved in instruction, but also a variety of simple, compound, and abstract resources. Many of the attacks on inequality in schools, and most of the legal challenges, have focused on spending per students, and sometimes on teachers measured by experience or credentials. But many compound, complex, and abstract resources are more unequally distributed than are simple resources—examples include spending per student, teacher salaries, and teacher certification and education—so equity issues cannot be remedied without addressing this large number of resources. Many of these resources are collective and require more than individual teachers acting independently. Recognizing a broad variety of resources is therefore crucial to understanding what makes schools effective, and understanding how unequally these resources are distributed creates an equity agenda that goes well beyond the search for more equal funding.

In Chapters 1 through 3 and in Chapter 5, we argued that many school reforms require a different kind of school, one we call *collective* to distinguish it from traditional schools and entrepreneurial schools. Collective schools require teachers, teacher-leaders, and school-level leaders who behave quite differently from those in traditional schools—more collaboratively and less hierarchically, in the pattern now widely known as distributed leadership, with collective responsibility for outcomes. To be sure, it's been difficult to prove that collective and collaborative schools are more effective (as it's difficult to prove anything in education). However, evidence about exemplary departments and on cohesive schools with internal accountability suggests that they are. Furthermore, traditional schools with isolated teachers and a greater emphasis on management than instruction have a hard time reforming themselves, partly because they cannot generate collective resources like improved instruction and a more supportive climate. School reorganization is therefore a prerequisite for reforms to enhance equity, another abstract resource that cannot be bought. To recapitulate a point from Chapter 1, borrowing from Robert Bellah, "we live through institutions" that can either facilitate or constrain the work of distributive equity.

Schools that attempt reform also need support from their districts and from state and federal policy—the subject of Chapters 4 and 5. Support includes funding, of course, and declining or unstable funding—especially the dismal conditions of the current fiscal crisis—makes it all but impossible for schools to plan well. However, support requires more than funding, and districts and states vary enormously in the extent to which they engage in capacity-building—in developing the ability of schools, and the teachers and leaders within them, to enhance effective resources. This observation implies, of course, that the entire structure of district, state, and federal policy-making is crucial to social justice, and once again that educators need to rely on institutions beyond the classroom and the school to achieve their goals. They can affect these policies in several ways, but particularly through disciplinary associations and through unions that promote the professional stature of teachers—the autonomy, the expertise, and the control of the instructional enterprise that are the foundations of professions in this country. Social justice unions, though relatively rare in the United States, can also play active roles not only in enhancing the professional status of teachers but also in promoting other dimensions of social justice.

Equity has been permanently on the education agenda since the 1960s and has been a primary motivation in school reform—for example, the demand in No Child Left Behind that all students be "proficient" by 2014. But in Chapter 5 we argued that there is more than one way to think about school reform. Most reforms have been top-down, initiated by districts or states—and increasingly the federal government—but they have been quite ineffective; for various reasons this pattern has led to what Larry Cuban calls "reforming again, again, and again," without real change. An alternative is to rely on school-initiated changes and inside-out practices, with reforms initiated by those at the school level who know best what students need and what their schools lack—the point of the "resource audit" in Tool 3-C. A shift to school-level reform does not mean that haphazard or seat-of-the-pants thinking will improve anything, however, so some of the same rational policy procedures—careful formulation of goals, a search for appropriate

solutions, the cycle of inquiry with its stages of evaluation and reformulation of policy, careful use of
evidence—are necessary, even though they have their
limitations. This school-centered approach to reform is
both a way of creating more democratic school communities and reform procedures and a way for schools to
put in place the methods to enhance equity that have
otherwise been so elusive.

The agenda for distributive justice therefore starts in
the classroom, with the elements of strong instruction
and with the personal relationships that often define good
teaching. But very quickly the attainment of equity shifts
from the classroom level to the school level—and then to
districts, states, the federal government, unions and their
ability to represent the professional interests of teachers,
and broader attitudes about education in this society. For
educators, all of these are connected, and all of them must
work together to achieve justice for all students.

**Cross-Reference
See Book 5 for
multiple
approaches to
promoting
equity in and
beyond the
classroom.**

DYNAMIC EQUITY

Conceptions of equity, like those in Tool 6-A, usually
measure differences among individuals or groups at one
point in time—they are *static* measures of equity. In contrast, when we consider the overall effects of schooling,
we need to recognize the *dynamic* process by which
people become educated over time. Children start formal
schooling, say at kindergarten, with unequal capacities,
both cognitive abilities (like knowledge of letters and
numbers, vocabulary, and sophistication of language)
and noncognitive capacities (like the ability to get along
with others, conceptions of what school is all about, and
patterns of interactions with adults)—the result of differences in family background as well as earlier forms of
schooling like early childhood programs. Equalizing
these initial differences might be the responsibility of
early childhood and family intervention programs like
Head Start, the Child Development Block Grant, and

other early childhood programs. Indeed, debate about providing universal access to early childhood education has become intense, and equalizing capacities before children start school has been a central rationale.

Then schools might narrow these initial differences, maintain them, or cause them to increase. In the United States, however, these differences appear to be magnified over time; for some of the evidence see Tool 6-B. Therefore, the growth patterns of high-, middle-, and low-performing students look something like the solid straight lines over grades K–8 in the graph, which diverge steadily between kindergarten and eighth grade. The result is that the differences among low-, medium-, and high-performing students become larger and larger over time. By the end of twelfth grade the variation is enormous: some have dropped out of school and are still reading at an elementary level whereas others are ready to go to the best colleges in the world.

Given evidence of diverging outcomes, an obvious question is, What causes growth trajectories to diverge rather than converge? This is a question that teachers and leaders in schools might answer for their own practices, particularly if they have the data on student outcomes over time. This is also a question that district and state personnel should answer, because a great deal of increasing inequality takes place *among* schools and *among* districts, not just within schools.

One of the most difficult aspects of dynamic inequality is that many explanations have been given for this pattern. One explanation focuses on the psychology of learning, specifically on the contention that "knowledge begets knowledge" (Resnick 1989)—implying that individuals with higher initial levels of learning are able to learn at a faster *rate* than others. A different explanation focuses on the continuing effects of family background. If aspects of families—like parental education, aspirations, or income—continue to reinforce or undermine schooling outcomes, then initial differences will continue to diverge over time because family background affects both initial differences and subsequent rates of learning and progress. In addition, nonschool influences like poor access to health care, lack of adequate nutrition, environmental pollutants, family stress including child abuse and neglect, the effects of parental mental illness, and neighborhood effects are likely to persist over a child's education (Berliner 2009), and may account for diverging trajectories and greater inequality over time.

School resources are often allocated by family background or race, in complex ways. High-socioeconomic-status students are more likely to live in districts with high spending and well-credentialed teachers; in contrast, poor and minority students are more likely to live in urban districts with uncredentialed teachers, overwhelmed administrators, and chaotic conditions. Stability—of students and teachers, principals and superintendents—is yet another abstract resource that may contribute to divergence, given the contrast between relatively stable suburban schools and many urban schools with instability of students, teachers, principals, and superintendents.

In addition, school resources are often allocated according to student performance. For example, the "best" teachers (or at least those with the most experience) usually choose to teach the "best" students, or honors and AP classes, or move to suburban schools with higher-performing students. Conversely, low-performing students are often assigned the most inexperienced teachers with the least seniority, or are assigned to low-ability, general, or vocational tracks with weaker teachers and lower expectations, or to general or vocational tracks with low teacher expectations, watered-down curricula, and unmotivated peers. Such allocations will reinforce high and low performance over time.

A particular resource that affects students over time includes grade-level norms, often embedded in state standards; these are mechanisms, along with grade-level textbooks, that might prevent divergence. Determining the grade level of teaching materials is difficult and tedious, but one effort to do so in an elementary school revealed that while all materials were on grade level in kindergarten and first grade, by second grade 23 percent of math materials and 20 percent of language arts materials were at first-grade level. The slippage became increasingly serious until by fifth grade 98 percent of both math and language arts materials were below grade level (Hollingsworth and Ybarra n.d.). If the material taught in some classes or schools falls further and further behind standards while teachers in other schools maintain grade-level norms, this exacerbates the divergence in learning.

Students' commitment to schooling may also contribute to divergence. Students with low levels of initial outcomes may become discouraged or shamed by their low performance whereas high-performing students are motivated by their success and further encouraged by parents and teachers. A special case of this explanation is the mistreatment of racial minority students: if African American, Latino, and American Indian students are subjected to slights or indifference or "micro-agressions," they may become increasingly discouraged or disconnected from schooling while their white and Asian American peers are supported and encouraged. As one concrete example, the process of dropping out of high school has often been described as a dynamic one where some students initially experience failure, become discouraged, don't exert as much effort, become increasingly attracted to distractions (such as television, games, and street life), suffer more failure, and begin a downward spiral of disengagement that ultimately ends in dropping out. Of course, schools contribute to these patterns when they provide unmotivating instruction, disparagement of low performance, or tracking into programs that are essentially dumping grounds. Conversely, stories of individual students finding a supportive teacher who encourages them to perform well are among the staples of the motivational literature. But without such interventions, differences in students' commitment to schooling may contribute to diverging outcomes.

Evidently, *many factors may contribute to divergence, and the solutions to these potential problems vary substantially. All of these possible explanations may operate to one degree or another; if all of them operate to some extent and reinforce one another—for example, as mediocre teaching and subtle mistreatment reinforce the disparities due to family background and low performance—this might explain why growth trajectories diverge so consistently.* It's difficult to know which of these many explanations are the most powerful, and therefore what solutions are most appropriate. But teachers and school leaders are in some ways in better positions than outsiders to understand what causes student performance to diverge in specific schools, so they should be part of the diagnosis.

Focus point

One more possibility is that trajectories might not be smooth and continuous, as they are on the left side of Tool 6-B. A good example is the transition from eighth to ninth grade. The lowest-performing students drop out or drift away by paying little attention to coursework; these students may fail to make any further progress. Other students, presumably those who have fallen behind but who still stay in school, are assigned to remedial courses or even special education, which tend to use the weakest forms of instruction—drill and repetition—on low-level content that bores and insults them, so remedial students fail to progress in high school content. Other low-performing students are relegated to general or traditional vocational tracks, where the curriculum is watered down, teachers have lower expectations of students, and peers have relatively low ambitions. At the upper end, high-performing students gain access to AP or honors tracks, and their rates of learning accelerate. These patterns lead to a burst or explosion of inequality from eighth to ninth grade, and then to progressively greater inequality over the high school years. When such a burst takes place, the likelihood of students catching up—on the trajectory labeled Intervention$_{hs}$ in Tool 6-B—seems virtually impossible, because the rate of learning required for catching up is so high. In addition, older students are more likely to become unmotivated by then, and adolescents often have things to do—some of them self-destructive—other than remain diligent students, so some students' lack of commitment to schooling may undermine even careful intervention efforts.

Such bursts of inequality from eighth to tenth to twelfth grade have been confirmed by W. Norton Grubb (2009), using data on test scores and aspirations over the high school years. Another such explosion may occur somewhere during the third or fourth grade, when schools shift from teaching basic competencies like reading and math to using these competencies to learn content. This creates widening differences between those who have mastered and those who have failed to master basic academic skills and school-appropriate behavior, sometimes referred to as the "fourth-grade slump." The transition to middle school, with a different pattern of teachers and subjects and often with formal tracking, may cause another such burst of inequality. Knowing that such transitions can cause greater inequality makes it possible to modify patterns of instruction and develop bridge programs to smooth these difficult transitions.

These ideas about dynamic inequality create a substantial agenda for reform, and for teachers and leaders committed to equity. In addition to strengthening early childhood programs, to reduce initial differences, *one class of solutions would focus on effective resources, and particularly on ensuring that they are consistently equalized from grade to grade. This is a reversal of the usual recommendation to concentrate improvements in the early grades, based on the theory that eliminating differences early on—in early childhood programs before kindergarten, and in the early grades—will prevent inequalities later on. But the*

Focus point

various causes of inequalities operate at all levels of the school system, and therefore creating equity over time requires consistent efforts to reduce differences in all grades. These resources include all those we reviewed in Chapter 3, particularly the various ways of eliminating the mistreatment of students of color, and instead supporting them with different methods drawn from culturally relevant pedagogy, multicultural education, different discipline policies, and the treatment of home languages.

A second category of correctives would include the ways that schools cope with students who have fallen behind grade-level norm, often called interventions. There are dozens and dozens of such interventions that schools have used, sometimes in the form of off-the-shelf curricula—each of them developed by individuals or groups that claim to have found the secret to accelerating learning (the new code word for remediation). In addition, many schools have tried intensification, or expanding the amount of learning time through after-school programs, zero-period classes, or double periods of math and English. Unfortunately, such interventions are often fragmented, in the sense that some low-performing students receive them while others do not; inconsistent, in that some students receive help in one grade but not in successive grades; and poorly connected to the regular classroom, so interventions may not focus on the subjects that give students the most trouble. Furthermore, the evaluations of most interventions are of poor quality, so it is unclear if interventions "work" even under the best of circumstances (Grubb 2009, ch. 8). *For teachers and teacher-leaders, a critical role is to scrutinize interventions more carefully, to ask how they are supposed to accelerate learning (i.e., their theory of action), and to determine whether they are consistent with other classroom practices.* Then, with the support of district and state policies (including better information about "what works"), it might be possible to bring low-performing students up to the trajectories of students on grade level.

Focus point

Finally, schools could anticipate transition points and other periods where there might be sudden bursts of inequality, rather than leaving the burden of adjustment to students and their parents. For example, an awareness of the "fourth-grade slump" can lead teachers to continue reinforcing basic skills for some students at the same time that they progress to upper-grade material. A few high schools have set up ninth-grade academies, or learning communities, that reinforce basic skills at the same time that students continue with the ninth-grade curriculum, rather than engaging in the usual "remedial pedagogy." Other schools have established bridge programs, sometimes taking place during the summer. With insights about the dynamic patterns of inequality, teachers and leaders can address some of the problems causing divergence in learning and progress.

However, some transitions cannot be easily smoothed by individual schools, and schools need to call on districts to provide transition mechanisms. Districts can more readily support the *multiple* schools that participate in transitions—middle schools and their feeder schools, for example, or high schools and the middle schools that send students to them. Districts can also incorporate information about transitions into guidance and counseling programs, getting students ready for the next step in their schooling. They can also create special transition programs (including summer programs) for students in need of support. The diverging trajectories that are caused by differences *among* districts require, by the same logic, state policy—returning us to the policies we examined in Chapter 4. But without a coordinated program of school practices, supportive district policies, and state and federal action, the differences among students are likely to increase year after year, leading to the enormous variation we see by the end of grade 12.

The American system of public schooling has not generally thought about equity in dynamic terms. Doing so presents substantial challenges, not only to think in new ways but also to develop new forms of data collection following students over time, new policies to ensure consistency over the grades, and new attention to transitions. And once again, equity in its dynamic sense requires teachers to think outside their classrooms, to understand the complex of factors that cause differences among students to diverge over time. Only with such understanding will it be possible to achieve equitable schools for all our children.

PROCEDURAL JUSTICE, FAIRNESS, AND DISCIPLINE

Given inequalities in access to schooling, funding, resources, or outcomes, most reforms operate under the assumption that democratic procedures—like the policies and reforms we covered in Chapters 4 and 5—can reduce inequalities through redistribution. However, the procedures creating schools are themselves inequitable (Young 2000). These structural inequalities and power relations are so deeply embedded that even supposedly democratic processes are biased toward those who are more powerful. For example, the procedures for registering to vote have been consistently embattled, with persistent evidence of racial biases even after the Voting Rights Act of 1964. The mechanisms for taxing citizens to support government services are inequitable in many ways, with many loopholes for the rich, and legions of tax lawyers fight to keep it that way. For public schools and other forms of education, it may seem obvious that teachers and administrators must have some forms of authority over students, particularly in enforcing the educational goals of schooling and in preparing children to be responsible citizens and community members. But necessary and legitimate power relations can easily be abused, and here is where injustice creeps in.

Key concepts
horizontal **and**
vertical equity

Within schools, where teachers are most involved, many forms of procedural justice involve student perceptions of fairness. Fairness often involves two simple conceptions of equity: **horizontal equity**, the idea that individuals who are alike should be treated alike, and **vertical equity**, the idea that individuals who are different should be treated differently. When students perceive that they are being treated differently from other students who, they think, are similar to them, or have engaged in similar behavior, they may label the situation unfair—for example, when one student is punished for something that another student got away with. Conversely, if two different students are treated the same despite their differences—if a student who did nothing is still punished because he was near a disturbance but did not participate in it—this too is unfair, a violation of vertical equity. Of course, teachers and administrators sometimes perceive students' behavior as different, meriting different treatment, when students think they are similar. But procedural injustice is an area where perceptions mean a great deal, and students respond best to procedures that they deem fair and consistent (Arum 2003). The lack of communication between teachers and students often prevents teachers from seeing the students' side and students from seeing the ways decisions get made.

Many cases of procedural injustice and horizontal inequity arise in discipline cases, where students perceive—correctly, it turns out—bias by race and class. For example, researchers found that African American students were more likely to be referred to the office by teachers, and for more subjective infractions like loitering and disrespect rather than clear violations of rules against smoking, vandalism, and cutting class (Skiba et al. 2002). Black students claimed that teachers were more likely to react to misbehavior on the part of black students, and these situations often provoked conflicts that escalated to referrals and suspensions. Suspensions from school constitute another area of procedural injustice: suspensions are commonly higher for males and for black or Latino students, and higher-performing students are less likely to be suspended for the same infractions (Noguera 2003). The irony here is dreadful: the lowest-performing students, who need more instructional time, are more likely to be suspended and miss school.

Although many schools have identified which *students* are responsible for referrals, the other side of such an analysis is to identify which *teachers* are responsible for referrals and suspensions. Often, a few teachers are responsible for a large proportion of disciplinary actions. The next step is to identify, through classroom observations, whether there is something about teachers' instruction or interactions with students that might explain high levels of referrals. In one case, a principal was able to determine that four teachers responsible for most referrals taught in the most rigid and traditional ways, were intolerant of any movement around the classroom, and interpreted rules in narrow and rigid ways—a good example of "principal research" (Mukerjee 2006). Thus, discipline problems may arise from an interaction of student and teacher behavior, and punishing students without changing teacher behavior may again be procedurally unfair.

Procedural injustice also lurks in differences *among schools* in their approaches to discipline. Zero-tolerance policies, in which every infraction is punished regardless of its severity, are disproportionately developed and enforced in schools serving low-income students of color (Skiba and Peterson 1999; Ayers, Dohrn, and Ayers 2001). In these cases an inequity exists *among* schools, and the result is that the parents of a white middle-class student in a suburban school might be called in for a meeting whereas a black working-class male might be suspended or expelled for the same infraction. Ann Ferguson's (2000) examination of an elementary school with these kinds of inequitable practices led to a concept

Cross-Reference
See Book 5, Chapter 4 for a related discussion of pedagogy and punishment.

that is useful in these discussions: teachers tend to "adul-
tify" the behavior of students of color, treating them not
as misbehaving children but as adults whose behavior is a
precursor to becoming criminals. Zero tolerance becomes especially draconian when schools use "School
Security Officers," sometimes from local police departments, to maintain order. Under these conditions behavior that might be dealt with as a school issue, potentially
with teachers as well as students to blame, ends up crimi-
nalizing student misbehavior. (In extreme cases, such
policies have resulted in truly outrageous situations, like
a six-year-old handcuffed for a temper tantrum, or two
students arrested for turning off the light in the girls'
bathroom.) And giving School Security Officers responsibility for discipline tends to focus on students and ab-
solve teachers from any complicity in behavior problems,
whereas behavior problems are often rooted in *teacher*
practices: in boring and unengaging teaching, in rigid
applications of rules, in disrespect of students, and in the
kinds of mistreatment we discussed in Chapter 3.

   Although procedural injustice seems particularly
prevalent in discipline issues, another arena in which procedural injustice is likely involves mechanisms for select-
ing students for different programs. (These are also
procedures that may determine inequality in school resources.) The processes for placing students into AP
classes have become controversial because they so often
select white middle-class students; in response, some
schools have instituted procedures whereby students can
choose to enroll in these classes without a selection mechanism. For a long time the procedures for placing students into traditional vocational tracks were seen as biased
against working-class students and students of color; the
procedures for placing students into special education
have been similarly challenged. Some large urban districts
assign students to high schools based on an application
procedure that favors more informed and better-
connected parents (Herszenhorn 2003), and similar

charges have been leveled against admissions to magnet schools and popular charter schools. The process of applying to college, including complex student aid procedures, is rife with violations of vertical equity: all students are treated the same, even though middle-class students can get more help from their parents (and sometimes from private college counselors) than can most working-class and immigrant students. The "solution" has been a patchwork of public and private efforts to provide better information and counseling to students who may lack support from their families, but these are inadequate given the institutional problem.

A third area of procedural injustice involves student rights to free speech and to procedural due process, and to freedom from search and seizure—all rights embedded in the Constitution. Many student rights cases arise when students are denied constitutional rights that adults would have, a form of horizontal inequity—unequal treatment of students and adults—that is particularly galling to adolescents on the verge of adulthood. As the Supreme Court declared in *Tinker v. Des Moines Independent School District*, "Students in school as well as out of school are 'persons' under the constitution. They are possessed of fundamental rights that the state must respect"—unless exercising these rights "materially and substantially" affects the operation of the school. In practice, then, the school's need for control and the students' rights may conflict, particularly in schools with strongly authoritarian views of the relationship between school and student (Cambron-McCabe 2009).

Procedural injustice operates at many levels, then: within classrooms and schools in conflicts among students, teachers, and administrators; in differences among schools; and in the procedures that determine the school resources that students can access. But procedural injustice operates in another way, by reinforcing a group's value or status within the hierarchy of education. When black students are overrepresented in suspensions or special education, or Latino students are more likely to be in remedial classes or the general track, or white middle-class students are more likely to be in AP classes or college-bound tracks, these procedural outcomes reinforce the high or low status of such groups of students (Lind and Tyler 1988). These quickly find their way into student perceptions of (un)fairness, which tend to break down along class and racial lines. For example, one study found that 90 percent of middle-class students felt that school discipline was basically fair while only 40 percent of low-income students did; low-income students were more likely to report being humiliated, yelled at, and ostracized, enhancing their alienation from school (Brantlinger 1991). These ways of reinforcing the low status of different groups mean that these groups perceive themselves as being treated unfairly, perceive teachers as arbitrary and hostile, and perceive school itself as an arena where they are unlikely to be successful. As Claude Steele (1997) might point out, these procedural injustices are precisely the actions that trigger "stereotype threat," where members of groups threatened by a group stereotype are likely to withdraw.

Once we are alerted to it, procedural injustice seems ubiquitous—so perhaps sensitivity to the problem is a first step in eradicating it. Schools have taken a number of steps to improve procedural justice, all of which require the active participation of teachers. One is to ensure that instruction is engaging and interactive; the best instruction is also the best form of classroom management. As John Dewey wrote nearly a century ago, schools are forced to keep order only "when the school is not a community held together by participation in common activities" (Dewey 1916, 55). Particularly with students of color, this may require including, as we have suggested at many points in this book, approaches to culturally relevant pedagogy and multicultural education that address racial and ethnic identities. Unfortunately, there is a general lack of understanding about pedagogical practices and the consequences for discipline. For example, most teachers do not understand what Geneva Gay (2000) calls "preambling"—the social need for African American males to establish community with each other as a way of engaging in any activity, including schooling. Allowing time for preambling would allow students to feel respected and to engage in schooling with a community of peers. Similarly, many teachers are unaware of norms of respect among young males, and their pedagogical corrections often cause what teachers then call defiance.

Perhaps the most common approach has tried to change the dynamics between students and teachers. Some of these are clearly behaviorist, as in systems of positive behavior intervention and support that provide incentives for students who exhibit positive behavior. It is common to believe that only extrinsic motivation will engage students of color and that they "need" behaviorist systems more. This results, for example, in some elementary schools where children are required to march from class to bathroom to recess without talking, often lining up in specific ways; in other schools, students join hands, walk in pairs, and use "inside" voices to have conversations—more consistent with preparing young people to behave as adults with behavior appropriate for different social settings. Other approaches identify the problem as one of school culture generally and provide teachers with preventive and proactive strategies—creating a school climate more respectful of students; promoting forms of mediation when students, or teachers and students, come into conflict; preparing teachers in methods of communication that defuse hostility instead of exacerbating it; introducing methods like restorative justice rather than continuing to depend on rules, conventional rewards, and punishments; and other ways of asserting the school's authority over students (Wolfgang 2005).

Similarly, collective schools can examine a broad range of policies beyond discipline that cause students to view schools as unfair. We cannot expect to prepare students to be citizens in a democracy without different kinds of classroom discourse, and we cannot expect to do that without looking at procedures within schools that are inequitable.

There are, then, many ways for teachers and teacher-leaders to be engaged in creating procedural justice, within their classrooms and their schools. All of them require teachers to be vigilant about the many forms that procedural injustice can take, and about their own behavior toward students. In addition, virtually all of them require collective action to resolve, because the problem is usually less one of individual teachers who are guilty of unfair treatment and more one of the basic culture of a school and its purpose in controlling students.

SOCIAL JUSTICE BEYOND SCHOOLING: COMPLEMENTARY NONEDUCATIONAL POLICIES

As we have noted throughout this book, schools exist not only within a system of district, state, and federal policies but also within a larger social and economic system, with noneducational policies that affect them in many ways. Families are themselves resources to schooling, and virtually every analysis—qualitative and quantitative—has found that dimensions of family background (or "class") affect schooling outcomes, particularly parental education, aspirations for children, and occupation. Other dimensions of student performance can be traced to health policy, when some students miss a great deal of schooling because of health problems (Berliner 2009, 11–14); to housing policies, where the lack of low-income housing causes some families to move frequently, disrupting their children's schooling (Rumberger and Larsen 1998); and to the lack of any urban policy, which leaves many urban neighborhoods crime-ridden, dilapidated, and unsafe. When we recognize that families and communities are potential resources for schooling rather than just deficits to be overcome, then improving the effectiveness and the equity of schooling also requires noneducational policies—not instead of but *in addition to* reforming schools. When we identify racial and ethnic disparities in schooling outcomes that cannot be explained away by other factors, then we should ask what racial and ethnic dimensions of existing school *and* nonschool policies might be to blame. Even though attention to nonschool policies often seems an afterthought, it would be irresponsible to ignore them just because they seem politically unattainable.

Unfortunately, "both/and" policies—both school reforms and changes to noneducational policies—have been difficult for educators to promote. One problem comes from rhetoric about "leaving no child behind" and the responsibility of educators to believe in the ability of all children to learn. Any educator who suggests that family effects, or the conditions of low-income communities, are partly to blame for some educational difficulties is criticized for making excuses, for being guilty of "another form of bias: the soft bigotry of low expectations," in George Bush's rebuke of educators. The position that educators have often blamed family background for school failure has some truth to it, but in its extreme form this criticism accuses anyone raising the serious problems of poverty and race of giving up on educational reform—which is not the case for most reformers.

A second problem has been the steady decline of the welfare state—the "safety net" programs providing income, food, housing, health care, and the other necessities of life for low-income families. The welfare state in this country has always been relatively weak. Consistent assaults have come from free marketeers, eager to sweep away any restrictions on markets; from corporations, happy for schools to provide them with workers but unwilling to pay for either the direct costs of schooling or the indirect costs necessary to make schooling more equitable; from anti-taxers, veiling their attacks on the welfare state with free-market rhetoric while they pass tax reductions for the rich, subsidies for corporations, and enormous public funding for the military and its unfounded wars (Krugman 2007). Ronald Reagan's administration stepped up efforts to diminish the welfare state; the attacks continued with a vengeance under a Republican Congress in the 1990s, and the administration of George W. Bush continued these assaults on the welfare state. For those who believe in supporting low-income children and their families, the past three decades have been disastrous. Anyone who promotes increases in programs for the poor—even in support of education—has been swimming against the tide.

Key concept
welfare state

(The **welfare state** is a term for those goods, services, and programs provided by governments that enhance the welfare of those without adequate earnings, health care, food, housing, or any of the other requirements of life. Broad conceptions of the welfare state usually include education and training as well.)

A third problem involves a change in the relationship between the welfare state and education policies. Increasingly, educational policies have been promoted as *substitutes* for a strong welfare state, rather than complements. For example, early childhood programs are usually advocated as ways to reduce the differences among children attributable to their families, rather than investing directly in families through income support programs or broader family policies. Those promoting education as preparation for occupations have characterized it as a cure for low incomes and inequality, especially among African Americans and Latinos. The War on Poverty of the 1960s was founded largely on education and job training, not on community development or labor market initiatives (which were enacted but were relatively weak). Most recently, when George W. Bush was asked in the 2004 presidential campaign about the widening gap between rich and poor, he responded with platitudes about education: "the No Child Left Behind Act is really a jobs act when you think about it." Other ideas promoting equity have collapsed: we no longer hear anything about a "family policy" to support families, a common proposal in the 1970s; or about public employment providing the unemployed with both training and employment while meeting social needs such as public housing, as we had in the 1970s; or about urban renewal, popular in the 1960s. Every big idea related to equity has been systematically snuffed out by antigovernment warriors in the past thirty years except for equality of educational opportunity—placing the burden on schools alone to achieve equity.

The alternative is to understand that a broad array of social policies are *complementary* to schooling, and that social justice requires *both* educational reforms *and* noneducational policies. In particular, such an approach would require the following:

- *Efforts to counter the effects of family background on schooling.* For example, early childhood policies, family literacy programs to orient parents and children to literacy practices associated with schooling, and certain forms of parent participation could moderate the effects of low parental education and aspirations for children, the most powerful family influences.
- *Housing policies to minimize the physical mobility of low-income students* whose parents have problems finding stable housing. Since mobility is detrimental to progress through schooling, housing subsidies and public housing should aim to maximize stability.
- *Income support policies* to help offset the effects of low income on learning and attending college. The specific ways to enhance incomes vary among advocates, but a long list of antipoverty mechanisms exists to choose from.

- *Labor market policies* to counter the extreme inequality in this country, documented in Tool
  1-B. These include more powerful minimum
  wage laws; real enforcement of existing antidiscrimination laws, forbidding either wage or
  employment discrimination against racial minorities and women; efforts to make workplaces
  easier to organize; and better accountability of
  highly paid managers to stockholders and regu-
  latory agencies (now starting to take place as a
  result of the economic crisis that began in
  2007).
- *A full range of health services,* so that poor health
  does not compromise a student's education. Indeed, reforming health care could be one of the
  most important equity policies for a wide range
  of citizens.
- *Mental health and social services,* so that low-
  income children have access to the programs
  that middle-income parents seek when their
  children are depressed, angry, antisocial, attracted to drugs or alcohol, or otherwise unable
  to participate in normal developmental stages.
  Such policies might enhance student commitment to schooling, which may otherwise be undermined by mental health issues.
- *Nutrition programs* that follow the well-
  accepted practices of school lunch and breakfast
  programs.
- *Urban development policies,* so that students are
  not surrounded by decay and violence.
- *Family support and child welfare programs* to reduce violence against and neglect of children,
  and to minimize the effects of mental health
  problems among parents.

Some of these services can be provided at schools, for example in the model of full-service schools providing a wide

array of social programs to their students or the model of community schools promoted by the Coalition of Community Schools. (See the suggested readings by Joy Dryfoos and James Comer and materials of the Coalition for Community Schools, http://www.communityschools .org.) But many noneducational policies—urban development, housing policies, income support—are far larger in scope than individual schools or districts can manage, and so a series of national policies is necessary in addition to support services at the school level.

In the early days of the Obama administration, there are many signs that safety net programs complementary to education may be strengthened. The stimulus package passed in early 2009 contained not only an additional $100 billion for educational improvement but also funds for various support programs, including health care for the poor, unemployment insurance benefits, grants to welfare and food stamp recipients, funds for affordable housing, homelessness prevention, and the redevelopment of foreclosed homes. President Barack Obama and Vice President Joe Biden promised to build a reliable safety net, particularly for those facing job transitions in a "fierce global economy," through portable health care, retirement savings accounts, and expanding unemployment insurance. How these proposals emerge from the political process remains to be seen, but at least the Obama administration has reversed the assaults on the welfare state through successive administrations from Reagan to Bush II.

At a more general level, the rhetoric about government's role has changed substantially. The fiscal crisis that started in 2007 has clarified that unregulated markets work poorly, that firms cannot be trusted to serve the public interest, and that the free-market rhetoric dominating policy-making since the 1970s is misleading and dangerous. The votes for Obama and public support for the 2009 stimulus package are signs of support for a more active government, a view that government can offer solutions to social issues rather than being just part of the problem. The reassessment of government has begun, as books like Paul Krugman's *The Conscience of a Liberal* (2007) and Jeff Madrick's *The Case for Big Government* (2009) argue strenuously against the view that government should be kept as small as possible. In many ways, the current economic and fiscal crisis has precipitated fundamental changes in how we look at all the institutions that affect us, including the welfare state, corporations and their regulation, and government. For public education, and for the noneducational policies that support equity in schooling, these are promising changes.

For teachers, teacher-leaders, and other school and district leaders, these fundamental changes provide new opportunities for participating in debates about noneducational policies. For secondary teachers in particular, these policies can become the subject of a more relevant social studies and history curriculum for students who are personally affected by these policies; students who understand their reality as a structural issue are more likely to engage in school and not feel a sense of personal discouragement (O'Connor, 1999). Either directly or through unions, educators can add their voices to those of other community organizers—health advocates, housing advocates, antipoverty warriors, and urban reformers. If teachers, with their numbers and vocal unions, could be consistently counted among the supporters of these approaches, that would add substantially to the constituency for equity policies. And educators have a particularly principled argument to make: that schooling, which is widely accepted as the foundation of a strong democracy and a vibrant economy, requires these noneducational policies to be as effective and equitable as possible. Education doesn't start at the classroom door, and the conditions for effective and equitable education are not found in schools only—so we need *both* school reforms *and* reforms of complementary policies if we are to realize the dreams we have for public education.

THE SCOPE OF THE SOCIAL JUSTICE AGENDA

The agenda we have outlined in this chapter is admittedly vast. It encompasses reforms across all levels of the educational system, from the classroom to the district and state to national policies. It encompasses forms of equity, like dynamic equity as students progress from year to year, that have rarely been considered. It extends well beyond schooling practices to the variety of noneducational policies outlined in the previous section. It may seem overwhelming, especially to beginning teachers who are finding challenge enough learning how to manage their own classrooms and become effective teachers. We are not suggesting that new teachers can take on active roles in their schools, districts, or unions right away; they can contribute to equity and effectiveness in other ways, by developing their own teaching practices and participating in the decisions of a collective school. But we hope that teachers can take a long-range view of their development: as they become adept in their own classrooms, they can begin to transfer their expertise to participation in teacher leadership, or in district activities, or in more active participation in unions or disciplinary associations.

Teachers can take a long-range view of their development.

It shouldn't be surprising that the social justice agenda is so large and complex. One consequence of living in a country that is diverse in many different ways *and* is highly inequitable is that inequalities have multiple and insidious ways of affecting everyone. Children walk into their classrooms with some of these influences, including the effects of their parents' education and home language, their understanding of what schooling is and how it fits into their opportunities, and the ambitions they have for their own schooling, occupations, and intellectual development. Other inequities are created within schools, in the differences among teachers and in institutional practices like tracking, and in the distribution of resources (broadly understood, as in Chapter 3). Still others are caused by fiscal limits, when schools cannot find the money for extensive after-school programs, effective interventions, or high-quality tutoring. Social attitudes are part of the mix, too: the attitudes toward working-class children, toward racial minority and immigrant students—indeed, toward all children who differ from middle-class white children—have been with us for a long time, and these attitudes infiltrate the classroom in many ways. And though an equity agenda could be more forcefully supported by noneducational policies, as we argued in the previous section, schools are still the central institution for expanding the opportunities of the next generation.

Our conception of schooling also requires a trade-off. On the one hand, it suggests that teachers and leaders can take on novel roles. It requires that they think beyond the classroom, that they recognize how much of what takes place within the classroom is the result of policies and institutional practices originating far outside classrooms. It may require more work—attending not only to classroom responsibilities but also to school responsibilities; serving on decision-making committees; participating actively in the direction of the school (as implied by the concept of "distributed leadership"); and playing more active roles as members of unions, disciplinary associations, and other groups pressing for equity in an inequitable society.

On the other hand, this vision of schooling provides a greater variety of roles for teachers, outside the classroom as well as inside, with the guiding proposition that moving from inside the classroom and school out is fundamentally more successful than what comes from the outside in. It provides teachers with more meaningful work, and more control over the conditions of their work, as schools become places where teachers participate in the meaningful decisions. It offers real professional standing, as teachers and teacher-leaders become recognized as individuals who are crucial not only to daily instruction but also to school improvement, the reconstruction of district and state policies, and wider advocacy for children in all areas of their lives. And if it were possible to sustain this vision, it might create a virtuous circle in which teachers are increasingly respected for their work, the higher status and independence of teaching draw more individuals into the field, and the conditions of teaching continue to improve—instead of the teacher-bashing that is now so common.

We ask so much of our schools in this country. Ever since the nineteenth century, schools have been seen as a panacea, capable of fixing all kinds of individual and social problems. This pattern continues now, in looking to education to provide individual opportunities for advancement, the solutions to inequality and poverty, and the conditions for international competitiveness and growth. But schools cannot deliver on the enormous expectations we have for them unless they can become more effective and more equitable. This requires new kinds of schools and new kinds of teachers and leaders. We have called these *collective* schools, and they are also collaborative, professional, and democratic. They entail new kinds of teachers and leaders, new ways of organizing decision-making within schools, new approaches to district and state policy, and new attitudes toward funding and resources in schools. These are institutional structures within which the people who give life to schools—eager students, involved parents, active teachers, committed principals—can all work more effectively and collaboratively. So, to return to the point we began Chapter 1 with, schools are not just about people—they are about people working within institutions that promote their best efforts.

DISCUSSION QUESTIONS

1. Of the various inequalities in the distribution of access, funding, resources, or outcomes, which are the most serious in your school? Which are the easiest to remedy? The hardest to remedy? Which of them can be corrected within the school? Which require corrections from district, state, or federal policy?

2. Where do your students perceive unfairness in the decision-making procedures in your school? What are the alternative solutions?

3. What kinds of noneducational policies would make the most difference to your students and your school? Where are the leverage points for changing these policies?

4. As you contemplate your career as a teacher, which roles outside of the classroom are most appealing? How would they draw on your experience as a teacher, and, in turn, how might they improve the conditions of classrooms?

5. There are many conceptions of equity, as Tool 6-A makes clear. In your school, is there a particular conception of equity that dominates, even if implicitly? You might think about how decisions get made regarding which teachers are assigned to which students; whether certain groups of students get "extra" resources, including interventions or special counseling; and whether there are any special efforts to address racial and ethnic gaps in achievement or progress.

FURTHER READING

Berliner, David. 2009. *Poverty and Potential: Out-of-School Factors and School Success*. Boulder, CO, and Tempe, AZ: Education and the Public Interest Center & Educational Policy Research Unit. Available at http://epicpolicy .org/publication/poverty-and-potential.

Blank, Martin, Amy Berg, and Atelia Melaville. 2006. *Community and Family Engagement: Principals Share What Works*. Washington, DC: Institute for

Educational Leadership. Available at http://www.iel.org.programs/ccs
.html.

Comer, James. 1996. *Rallying the Whole Village: The Comer Process for Reforming Education.* New York: Teachers College Press.

Dryfoos, Joy. 1994. *Full-Service Schools: A Revolution in Health and Social Services for Children, Youth, and Families.* San Francisco: Jossey-Bass.

Krugman, Paul. 2007. *The Conscience of a Liberal.* New York: W. W. Norton.

Madrick, Jeff. 2009. *The Case for Big Government.* Princeton, NJ: Princeton University Press.

Rothstein, Richard. 2004. *Class and Schools: Using Social, Economic, and Educational Reform to Close the Black-White Achievement Gap.* New York: Economic Policy Institute.

TOOL 6-A: MULTIPLE CONCEPTS OF EQUITY: THE "LANDSCAPE" OF EQUITY AND INEQUALITY

In this country, we sometimes have a hard time distinguishing between equity and equality. Equity is a normative concept, expressing what education individuals *ought* to receive; inequality and equality are descriptive, describing what good things they *do* receive. Equality (of money or resources, for example) may not be equitable if we believe that some high-need students merit more money or resources than others.

Several conceptions of equity have developed historically in this country, including a *lack of barriers* based on race, class, gender, or other attributes; *equality*, meaning that all individuals have the same amount of something; *neutrality*, meaning that all groups have the same average amount of something, even if there is variation among members of each group; *adequacy*, or providing a basic minimum to all individuals; and *compensatory policies,* where the least advantaged receive more of something (Pole 1978).

We can apply these concepts of equity to *access*, the most basic aspect of schooling (whether a student can participate in a school or not); to *funding*, the subject of so many court cases; to the *school resources* that money might be able to buy; or to *outcomes,* like learning and test scores, high school completion, or values. If we apply these five conceptions of equity to four dimensions of education, then the following "landscape" of equity conceptions results. These conceptions of equity are not necessarily consistent with one another: for example, the concept of equal treatment precludes compensatory policies, and adequacy is unlikely to lead to either equality or neutrality.

Examine the "landscape" of equity conceptions, and examine some of the equity practices in your school. Clarify how your statements about *inequity* are backed up by evidence of *inequality*. See if you can develop a consensus about which forms of equity are most important in your school, and which have been largely ignored.

Conceptions of Equity	Applied to Access	Applied to Funding	Applied to Resources	Applied to Outcomes
Noah Webster: "No barriers"	1. Policies of inclusion: special education, desegregation by race, gender	2. Neutrality-oriented school finance cases	3. Policies of inclusion applied to special programs (like AP); language policies for ELL students	4. Affirmative action
Andrew Jackson: "No artificial distinctions": equality	5. The common school movement	6. *Serrano*; equality of funding; district efforts to eliminate intra-school inequality	7. Kozol, *Savage Inequalities*; equal resources for counselors and specialists	8. Radical egalitarians
Andrew Jackson: "No artificial distinctions": neutrality	9. No differences (of gender, race, etc.) in AP or honors courses, in high-status majors	10. Wealth neutrality; income neutrality; racial neutrality in funding	11. Equity in the allocation of qualified teachers	12. No achievement gaps by race or gender; no ethnic or class variation in high school dropout rates
Adequacy	13. Minimum school standards; accreditation standards in postsecondary education	14. Adequacy 1[a] and 2[b]; foundation formulas	15. *Williams*; class size reduction; "qualified teachers" in NCLB; state interventions for low-performing schools	16. Adequacy 3[c]; minimum standards in NCLB; state exit exams
"Policies of correction"	17. Affirmative action for entry into elite public high schools and postsecondary education	18. Compensatory education; weighted student pupil formulas	19. Compensatory education; early childhood programs; allocation of the best teachers to lowest-performing students	20. Affirmative action for PSE access; set-sides for minority- and female-owned businesses; Vonnegut, *Player Piano*[d]

[a] Adequacy 1 is the spending levels of districts or schools with high levels of performance.

[b] Adequacy 2 is the spending necessary for specific resources (qualified teachers, certain pupil/teacher ratios, sufficient textbooks, etc.) that professionals judge to be adequate (the professional judgment method).

[c] Adequacy 3 is a level of spending sufficient to bring all students to some adequate level of outcomes, which itself needs to be defined.

[d] In *Player Piano*, Kurt Vonnegut describes a world in which individual gifts are countered by socially imposed limits. For example, especially intelligent individuals have their thoughts interrupted by electrical impulses every 30 seconds; especially graceful dancers are weighted down with sandbags.

TOOL 6-B: ANALYZING DYNAMIC INEQUALITY

The following diagram is intended to describe schooling outcomes over time. The outcomes might be test scores, or more abstract dimensions like attitudes or commitment to schooling, or ambitions, such as educational or occupational aspirations. In practice there are few measures that can be collected over thirteen years of schooling, so this graph may be useful more in thinking about differences among students than in measuring them over long periods of time.

The existing evidence indicates that inequalities among students do become larger over time. Roland Fryer and Steven Leavitt (2005) show that modest black-white differences in kindergarten increase until the spring of third grade. Meredith Phillips, James Crouse, and John Ralph (1998) estimate that initial black-white differences increase until they are two to four times as large by the end of grade 12, as measured by vocabulary tests. Charles Hargis (2006, fig. 1) shows how scores on the Peabody Individual Achievement Test widen steadily over time. Russell Rumberger and Patricia Gándara (2004) found that English-language learners are one and one-half grade levels behind native English speakers by grade 5, two years behind by grade 8, and four and one-half years behind by grade 11. Norton Grubb (2009, ch. 6) found that differences in test scores widen steadily between grades 8, 10, and 12, with these differences associated with family background, a variety of school resources, and measures of a student's commitment to schooling.

Think about the practices in your school, and in schools in general, that might cause these growth trajectories to diverge and to "explode" at certain points (here, the transition to high school). What can be done to prevent these trajectories from diverging? What can you do within your school? What requires district or state policies? And what noneducational policies might be necessary as well?

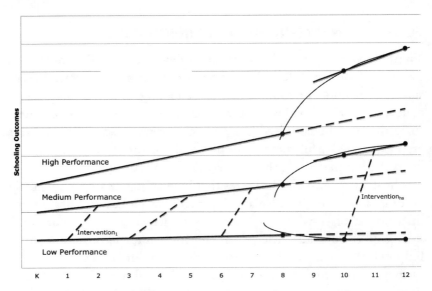

FIGURE 6.1. Potential growth trajectories

REFERENCES AND FURTHER READING

ACLU Foundation of Southern California and Public Advocates, Inc. 2007. *Williams v. California: The Statewide Impact of Two Years of Implementation.* Los Angeles: ACLU Foundation.

Anyon, Jean. 1997. *Ghetto Schooling: A Political Economy of Urban Educational Reform.* New York: Teachers College Press.

Argyris, Chris, and Donald Schon. 1978. *Organizational Learning: A Theory of Action Perspective.* Reading, MA: Addison-Wesley.

Arum, Richard. 2003. *Judging School Discipline: The Crisis of Moral Authority.* Cambridge, MA: Harvard University Press.

Austin, James, Allen Grossman, Robert Schwartz, and Jennifer Suesse. 2006. "Long Beach Unified School District: Change That Leads to Improvement." PEL-006. Cambridge, MA: Public Education Leadership Project, Harvard University. Available at http://www.hbsp.harvard.edu.

Ayers, William, Bernardine Dohrn, and Rick Ayers. 2001. *Zero Tolerance: Resisting the Drive for Punishment in Our Schools.* New York: New Press.

Ball, Stephen J. 1987. *The Micropolitics of School.* New York: Routledge.

Banks, James, and Cherry McGee Banks, eds. 2004. *Handbook of Research on Multicultural Education.* San Francisco: Jossey-Bass.

Barth, Roland. 1990. *Improving Schools from Within: Teachers, Parents, and Principals Can Make a Difference.* San Francisco: Jossey-Bass.

———. 2003. *Lessons Learned: Shaping Relationships and the Culture of the Workplace.* Thousand Oaks, CA: Corwin Press.

———. 2007. "What Is Instructional Leadership?" *Educational Leadership,* December–January 2007–2008.

Bellah, Robert, Richard Madsen, Steve Tipton, William Sullivan, and Ann Swidler. 1985. *Habits of the Heart: Individualism and Commitment in American Life.* Berkeley: University of California Press.

————. 1991. *The Good Society.* New York: Knopf.

Berliner, David. 2009. *Poverty and Potential: Out-of-School Factors and School Success.* Boulder, CO, and Tempe, AZ: Education and the Public Interest Center & Educational Policy Research Unit. Available at http://epic policy.org/publication/poverty-and-potential.

Blank, Martin, Amy Berg, and Atelia Melaville. 2006. *Community and Family Engagement: Principals Share What Works.* Washington, DC: Institute for Educational Leadership.

Boaler, Jo, and Megan Staples. 2008. "Creating Mathematical Futures through an Equitable Teaching Approach: The Case of Railside School." *Teachers College Record* 110, 3: 608–645.

Bodilly, Susan, and Martin Beckett. 2005. *Making Out-of-School-Time Matter: Evidence for an Action Agenda.* Santa Monica, CA: RAND Corporation.

Bransford, John D., A. L. Brown, and Rodney R. Cocking. 1999. *How People Learn: Brain, Mind, Experience, and School.* Washington, DC: National Academy Press.

Brantlinger, E. 1991. "Social Class Distinctions in Adolescents' Reports of Problems and Punishment in School." *Behavioral Disorders* 17, 1: 36–46.

Brill, Fred. 2009. *Leading and Learning: Effective School Leadership Through Reflective Inquiry.* Portland, ME: Stenhouse.

Brophy, Jerome. 1990. "Effective Schooling for Disadvantaged Students." *Better Schooling for the Children of Poverty: Alternatives to Conventional Wisdom,* vol. 3. U.S. Department of Education, Office of Planning Budget and Evaluation.

Brown, Jitu, Eric Gutstein, and Pauline Lipman. 2009. "Arne Duncan and the Chicago Success Story: Myth or Reality?" *Rethinking Schools Online* 23, 3. Available at http://www.rethinkingschools.org/archive/23_03/arne233.shtml.

Bryk, Anthony, and Barbara Schneider. 2002. *Trust in Schools: A Core Resource for Improvement.* New York: Russell Sage Foundation.

Calkins, Andrew, William Guenther, Grace Belfiore, and Dave Lash. 2007. *The Turnaround Challenge: Supplement to the Main Report.* Boston: Insight Education and Research Institute.

Cambron-McCabe, Nelda. 2009. "Balancing Students' Constitutional Rights." *Phi Delta Kappan* 20, 20: 709–713.

Carnoy, Martin, Richard Elmore, and Leslie Siskin, eds. 2003. *The New Accountability: High Schools and High-Stakes Testing.* New York: Routledge.

Center for Research on Education Outcomes. 2009. *Multiple Choice: Charter School Performance in 16 States.* Stanford, CA: Stanford University Press.

Christensen, Linda. 2006. "Portrait Poems: Stepping into the World of Others." In Enid Lee, Deborah Menkart, and Margo Okazawa-Rey, eds., *Beyond*

Heroes and Holidays: A Practical Guide to K–12 Anti-Racist, Multicultural Education, and Staff Development. Washington, DC: Teaching for Change.

Cohen, David, and Deborah Ball. 1993. "Pedagogy and Policy." In David Cohen, Milbrey McLaughlin, and Joan Talbert, eds., *Teaching for Understanding: Challenges for Policy and Practice.* San Francisco: Jossey-Bass.

Comer, James. 1996. *Rallying the Whole Village: The Comer Process for Reforming Education.* New York: Teachers College Press.

Cuban, Larry. 1988. *The Managerial Imperative and the Practice of Leadership in School.* Albany: State University of New York Press.

———. 1990. "Reforming Again, Again, and Again." *Educational Researcher* 19, 3: 313.

———. 1993. *How Teachers Taught: Constancy and Change in American Classrooms, 1880–1990,* 2nd ed. New York: Teachers College Press.

Deschenes, Sarah, Larry Cuban, and David Tyack. 2001. "Mismatch: Historical Perspectives on Schools and Students Who Don't Fit Them." *Teachers College Record* 103: 525–547.

Dewey, John. 1916. *Democracy and Education: An Introduction to the Philosophy of Education.* New York: Macmillan.

———. 1938. *Experience and Education.* New York: Simon and Schuster.

Donovan, M. Suzanne, and John Bransford, eds. 2005. *How Students Learn: History, Mathematics, and Science in the Classroom.* Washington, DC: National Academies Press.

Dreeben, Robert. 1968. *On What Is Learned in Schools.* Reading, MA: Addison Wesley.

Dryfoos, Joy. 1994. *Full-Service Schools: A Revolution in Health and Social Services for Children, Youth, and Families.* San Francisco: Jossey-Bass.

DuFour, Rebecca, Robert Eaker, and Gayle Karhanek. 2004. *Whatever It Takes: How Professional Learning Communities Respond When Kids Don't Learn.* Bloomington, IN: National Education Service.

Dutro, Susana. 2007. *A Focused Approach to Instruction for English Learners.* Available online at http://www.elachieve.

Dutro, Susana, and Carrol Moran. 2003. "Rethinking English Language Instruction: An Architectural Approach." In Eugene Garcia, ed., *English Learners: Reaching the Highest Level of English Literacy.* Newark, DE: International Reading Association.

Elmore, Richard. 2004. "When Accountability Knocks." In *School Reform from the Inside Out.* Cambridge, MA: Harvard Education Press.

Eubanks, Eugene, Ralph Parish, and Dianne Smith. 1997. "Changing the Discourse in Schools." In Peter Hall, ed., *Race, Ethnicity and Multicultural Policy and Practice.* New York: Garland Publishing.

Farkas, George, and L. Shane Hall. 2000. "Can Title I Achieve Its Goal?" In Diane Ravitch, ed., *Brookings Papers on Education Policy 2000.* Washington, DC: Brookings Institution Press.

Ferguson, Ann. 2000. *Bad Boys: Public Schools in the Making of Black Masculinity.* Ann Arbor: University of Michigan Press, 2000.

Freire, Paulo. 1970. *The Pedagogy of the Oppressed.* New York: Continuum.

Fryer, Roland, and Steven Leavitt. 2005. "The Black-White Test Score Gap Through Third Grade." NBER Working Paper 11049. Cambridge, MA: National Bureau of Economic Research.

Fullan, Michael. 2007. *The New Meaning of Educational Change.* New York: Teachers College Press.

Fuller, Bruce, Joseph Wright, Karen Gesicki, and Erin Kang. 2007. "Gauging Growth: How to Judge No Child Left Behind?" *Educational Researcher* 36, 5: 268–278.

Gardner, Howard. 1983, revised 1993. *Frames of Mind: The Theory of Multiple Intelligences.* New York: Basic Books.

Gay, Geneva. 2000. *Culturally Responsive Teaching: Theory, Research, and Practice.* New York: Teachers College Press.

Gewertz, Catherine. 2007. "Miami 'Zone' Gives Schools Intensive Help." *Education Week* 27, 8 (October 17): 24–27.

Grubb, W. Norton. 2009. *The Money Myth: School Resources, Outcomes, and Equity.* New York: Russell Sage Foundation.

Grubb, W. Norton, and Marvin Lazerson. 2004. *The Education Gospel: The Economic Roles of Schooling.* Cambridge, MA: Harvard University Press.

Gutierrez, Rochelle. 2000. "Advancing African-American, Urban Youth in Mathematics: Unpacking the Success of One Math Department." *American Journal of Education* 109, 1: 63–111.

Hakuta, Kenji, and Herlinda Cancino. 1977. "Trends in Second Language Acquisition Research." *Harvard Educational Review* 47: 294–316.

Hanushek, Eric A. 1989. "The Impact of Differential Expenditures on School Performance." *Educational Researcher* 18: 45–62.

Hargis, Charles. 2006. "Setting Standards: An Exercise in Futility?" *Phi Delta Kappan* 87, 5: 393–395.

Harris, Douglas. 2006. "Ending the Blame Game on Educational Equity: A Study of 'High Flying' Schools and NCLB." EPSL-0603-120-EPRU. Tempe: Educational Policy Research Unit, Arizona State University.

Heath, Shirley B. 1983. *Ways with Words: Language, Life, and Work in Communities and Classrooms.* New York: Cambridge University Press.

Herszenhorn, David. 2003. "Parents Perplexed by High School Admissions Rule." *New York Times,* October 24.

Hess, Frederick. 1999. *Spinning Wheels: The Politics of Urban School Reform.* Washington, DC: Brookings Institution.

———. 2006. *Tough Love for Schools: Essays on Competition, Accountability and Excellence.* Washington, DC: American Enterprise Institute.

Hollingsworth, John, and Silvia Ybarra. Undated. "Analyzing Classroom Instruction: Curriculum Calibration." DataWorks Educational Research, http://www.dataworks-ed.com.

Ingersoll, Richard. 2003. *Who Controls Teachers' Work? Power and Accountability in America's Schools.* Cambridge, MA: Harvard University Press.

Institute for Educational Science. 2008. *Reading First Impact Study: Interim Report.* NCES 2008-4016. Washington, DC: U.S. Department of Education.

Jacob, Brian. 2007. "The Challenges of Staffing Urban Schools with Effective Teachers." *Future of Children* 17, 1: 129–153.

Jerald, Craig D. 2001. *Dispelling the Myths Revisited: Preliminary Findings from a Nationwide Analysis of "High-Flying" Schools.* Washington, DC: Education Trust.

Kane, Thomas. 2004. *The Impact of After-School Programs: Interpreting the Results of Four Recent Evaluations.* New York: William T. Grant Foundation.

Katz, Michael, and Mark Stern. 2006. *One Nation Divisible: What America Is and What It Is Becoming.* New York: Russell Sage Foundation.

Kerchner, Charles, and Krista Caufman. 1993. "Building the Airplane While It's Rolling Down the Runway." In Charles Kerchner and Julia Koppich, eds., *A Union of Professionals: Labor Relations and Educational Reform.* New York: Teachers College Press.

Kerchner, Charles, and Julia Koppich. 1993. *A Union of Professionals: Labor Relations and Educational Reform.* New York: Teachers College Press.

Knapp, Michael, and Associates. 1995. *Teaching for Meaning in High-Poverty Classrooms.* New York: Teachers College Press.

Kozol, Jonathan. 1967. *Death at an Early Age: The Destruction of the Hearts and Minds of Negro Children in the Boston Public Schools.* Boston: Houghton Mifflin.

———. 1991. *Savage Inequalities: Children in America's Schools.* New York: HarperPerennial.

Krugman, Paul. 2007. *The Conscience of a Liberal.* New York: W. W. Norton.

Kruse, S., Karen Seashore Louis, and Anthony Bryk. 1994. *Building Professional Community in Schools.* Madison: Center on Organization and Restructuring of Schools, University of Wisconsin.

Ladson-Billings, Gloria. 2006. "From the Achievement Gap to the Education Debt: Understanding Achievement in U.S. Schools." *Educational Researcher* 35, 7: 3–12.

Lareau, Annette. 2003. *Unequal Childhoods: Class, Race, and Family Life.* Berkeley: University of California Press.

Lauer, P. A., M. Akiba, S. B. Wilkerson, H. A. Apthorp, D. Snow, and M. Martin-Glenn. 2003. *The Effectiveness of Out-of-School-Time Strategies in Assisting Low-Achieving Students in Reading and Mathematics.* Aurora, CO: Mid-continent Research for Education and Learning.

Legislative Research Commission. 2006. *Highly-Skilled Educator Program.* Research Report #339. Frankfort, KY: Program Review and Investigations Committee.

LeMoine, Noma. 2003. *English for Your Success Teacher Handbook: Academic English Mastery.* http://www.learnmedia.com/aemp/englishforyoursuccess .html.

Lemons, Richard, T. Luschel, and Leslie Siskin. 2003. "Leadership and the Demands for Standards-Based Accountability." In Martin Carnoy, Richard Elmore, and Leslie Siskin, eds., *The New Accountability: High Schools and High-Stakes Testing.* New York: Routledge.

Leonardo, Zeus. 2004. "The Color of Supremacy." *Educational Philosophy and Theory,* 32, 2: 137–152.

Lind, E. Allen, and Tom Tyler. 1988. *The Social Psychology of Procedural Justice: Critical Issues in Social Justice.* New York: Plenum Press.

Little, Judith Warren. 1981. "Norms of Collegiality and Experimentation: Workplace Conditions of School Success." *American Educational Research Journal* 19, 3: 325–340.

———. 2006. *Professional Development and Professional Community in the Learning-Centered School.* Washington, DC: National Education Association.

Losen, Daniel, and Gary Orfield, eds. 2002. *Racial Inequity in Special Education.* Cambridge, MA: Harvard Education Press.

Lynd, Robert, and Helen Lynd. 1929. *Middletown: A Study in American Culture.* New York: Harcourt, Brace, and World.

Madrick, Jeff. 2009. *The Case for Big Government.* Princeton, NJ: Princeton University Press.

Magnuson, Katharine, and Jane Waldfogel, eds. 2008. *Steady Gains and Stalled Progress: Inequality and the Black-White Test Score Gap.* New York: Russell Sage Foundation.

McDonald, Joseph P. 1996. *Redesigning School: Lessons for the 21st Century.* San Francisco: Jossey-Bass.

McDonnell, Lorraine M., and Richard F. Elmore. 1987. "Getting the Job Done: Alternative Policy Instruments." *Education Evaluation and Policy Analysis* 9, 2: 133–152.

McIntosh, Peggy. 1988. "Unpacking the Invisible Knapsack." www.case
.edu/president/aaction/UnpackingTheKnapsack.pdf.

Meier, Deborah. 1995. *The Power of Their Ideas: Lessons from a Small School in Harlem*. Boston: Beacon Press.

Minorini, Paul A., and Stephen D. Sugarman. 1999. "Educational Adequacy and the Courts: The Promise and Problems of Moving to a New Paradigm." In Helen F. Ladd, Rosemary Chalk, and Janet S. Hansen, eds., *Equity and Adequacy in Education Finance: Issues and Perspectives*. Washington, DC: National Academies Press.

Minow, Martha. 1997. *Not Only For Myself: Identity, Politics, and Law*. New York: New Press.

Molnar, Alex, David Garcia, Gary Miron, and Shannon Berry. 2007. *Profiles of For-Profit Education Management Organizations: 2006–2007*. Tempe: Commercialism in Education Research Unit, Education Policy Studies Laboratory, Arizona State University.

Moore, Susan, Morgan L. Donaldson, Mindy Sick Munger, John P. Papay, and Emily Kalejs Qazibash. 2007. *Leading the Local: Teachers Union Presidents Speak on Change, Challenges*. Washington, DC: Education Sector.

Mukerjee, Diane. 2006. "Why Are African American Students Over-Represented in Behavioral Referral Data at Stoneman Elementary School?" Unpublished paper. Berkeley: School of Education, University of California.

National Research Council, Committee on Increasing High School Students' Engagement and Motivation to Learn. 2004. *Engaging Schools: Fostering High School Students' Motivation to Learn*. Washington, DC: National Academies Press.

Nelson, F. H., E. Muirt, and N. Meter. 2001. "Public Money and Privatization in K–12 Education." In S. Chaikind and W. Fowler, eds., *Education Finance in the New Millennium: AEFA 2001 Yearbook*. Larchmont, NY: Eye on Education.

Newmann, Frank, Anthony Bryk, and Jenny Nagoaka. 2001. *Authentic Intellectual Work and Standardized Tests: Conflict or Coexistence?* Chicago: Consortium on Chicago School Research, University of Chicago.

Newmann, Fred M., Betty Ann Smith, Elaine Allensworth, and Anthony S. Bryk. 2001. "Instructional Program Coherence: What It Is and Why It Should Guide School Improvement Policy." *Educational Evaluation and Policy Analysis* 23, 4: 297–321.

Nickell, Stephen. 2004. "Poverty and Worklessness in Britain." *Economic Journal* 114: C1–C25.

Noguera, Pedro. 1995. "Preventing and Producing Violence: A Critical Analysis of Responses to School Violence." *Harvard Educational Review* 65, 2: 189–212.

————. 2003. "Schools, Prisons, and Social Implications of Punishment: Rethinking Disciplinary Practices." *Theory into Practice* 42, 4: 341–350.

Oakes, Jeannie. 2004. "Education Inadequacy, Inequality, and Failed State Policy: A Synthesis of Expert Reports Prepared for *Williams v. California.*" *Teachers College Record* 106, 10: 1889–1906.

Oakes, Jeannie, and Marisa Saunders. 2008. *Beyond Tracking: Multiple Pathways to College and Careers.* Cambridge, MA: Harvard Education Press.

O'Connor, Carla. 1999. "Race, Class, and Gender in America: Narratives of Oppportunity Among Low-Income African-American Youths." *Sociology of Education* 72 (July): 137–157.

Olsen, Brad. 2008. "Introducing Teacher Identity." *Teacher Education* 35, 3 (Summer): 3–6.

Olsen, Brad, and Dena Sexton. 2009. "Threat Rigidity, School Reform, and How Teachers View Their Work Inside Current Education Policy Contexts." *American Education Research Journal* 46, 1: 9–24.

Peterson, Bob, and Michael Charney. 1999. *Transforming Teacher Unions: Fighting for Better School and Social Justice.* Milwaukee, WI: Rethinking Schools.

Phillips, Meredith, James Crouse, and John Ralph. 1998. "Does the Black-White Test Score Gap Widen After Children Enter School?" In Christopher Jencks and Meredith Phillips, eds., *The Black-White Test Score Gap.* Washington, DC: Brookings Institution.

Pole, J. R. 1978, reprinted 1994. *The Pursuit of Equality in American History.* Berkeley: University of California Press.

Powell, Arthur, Eleanor Farrar, and David Cohen. 1985. *The Shopping Mall High School: Winners and Losers in the Educational Marketplace.* Boston: Houghton Mifflin.

Pressman, Jeffery, and Aaron Wildavsky. 1979. *Implementation: How Great Expectations in Washington Are Dashed in Oakland: or, Why It's Amazing That Federal Programs Work at All, This Being a Saga of the Economic Development Administration as Told by Two Sympathetic Observers Who Seek to Build Morals on a Foundation of Ruined Hopes.* Berkeley: University of California Press.

Puma, Michael J., Nancy Karweit, Cristofer Price, Anne Ricciuti, William Thompson, and Michael Vaden-Kiernan. 1997. *Prospects: Final Report on Student Outcomes.* Washington, DC: U.S. Department of Education, Planning and Evaluation Service.

Quint, Janet. 2006. *Meeting Five Critical Challenges of High School Reform.* New York: MDRC.

Reeves, Douglas B. 2004. *Accountability in Action: A Blueprint for Learning Organizations.* Englewood, CO: Advanced Learning Press.

———. 2009. "Discovering the 'Secrets' of High Poverty, High Success Schools." Available at http://www.teachersofcolor.com/2009/04/uncovering-the-secrets-of-high-poverty-high-successschools.

Resnick, Lauren, ed. 1989. *Knowing, Learning, and Instruction: Essays in Honor of Robert Glaser.* Hillsdale, NJ: Lawrence Erlbaum Associates.

Rose, Mike. 2006. *Possible Lives: The Promise of Public Education in America.* New York: Penguin Books.

Rothstein, Richard. 2004. *Class and Schools: Using Social, Economic, and Educational Reform to Close the Black-White Achievement Gap.* New York: Economic Policy Institute.

Roza, Marguerite, and Paul Hill. 2006. "How Can Anyone Say What's Adequate If Nobody Knows How Money Is Spent Now?" In Eric Hanushek, ed., *Courting Failure: How School Finance Lawsuits Exploit Judges' Good Intentions and Harm Our Children.* Palo Alto, CA: Hoover Press.

Rumberger, Russell, and Patricia Gándara. 2004. "Seeking Equity in the Education of California's English Learners." *Teachers College Record* 106, 10: 2032–2056.

Rumberger, Russell, and Katherine Larson. 1998. "Student Mobility and the Increased Risk of High School Dropout." *American Journal of Education Research* 107: 1–35.

Schmoker, Michael. 1999. *The Key to Continuous School Improvement.* Alexandria, VA: Association for Supervision and Curriculum Development.

Scott, Janelle. 2008. "Managers of Choice: Race, Gender, and the Political Ideology of the 'New' Urban School Leadership." In W. Feinberg and C. Lubienski, eds., *School Choice Policies and Outcomes: Philosophical and Empirical Perspectives on Limits to Choice in Liberal Democracies.* Albany: State University of New York Press.

Senge, Peter. 1990. *The Fifth Discipline: The Art and Practice of the Learning Organization.* New York: Doubleday.

Shavelson, Richard, and Lisa Towne, eds. 2002. *Scientific Research in Education.* Washington, DC: National Academies Press.

Sirin, Selcuk. 2005. "Socioeconomic Status and Academic Achievement: A Meta-Analytic Review of the Research." *Review of Educational Research* 75, 3: 417–453.

Skiba, R., and R. Peterson. 1999. "The Dark Side of Zero Tolerance: Can Punishment Lead to Safe Schools?" *Phi Delta Kappan* 80, 5: 372–382.

Skiba, R., R. Michael, A. Nardo, and R. Peterson. 2002. "The Color of Discipline: Sources of Racial and Gender Disproportionality in School Punishment." *Urban Review* 34, 4: 4–19.

Smith, James, and Finis Welch. 1986. *Closing the Gap: Forty Years of Economic Progress for Blacks.* Santa Monica, CA: RAND.

Snow, Catherine, Susan M. Burns, and Peg Griffin. 1998. *Preventing Reading Difficulties in Young Children.* Washington, DC: National Academies Press.

Solorzano, Daniel. 2001. "Critical Race Theory, Racial Microaggressions, and the Experience of Chicana and Chicano Scholars." *Qualitative Inquiry* 8: 23–44.

Spillane, James. 2006. *Distributed Leadership.* San Francisco: Jossey-Bass.

Spillane, James, and John B. Diamond, eds. 2007. *Distributed Leadership in Practice.* New York: Teachers College Press.

Spillane, James, Richard Halverson, and John B. Diamond. 2001. "Investigating School Leadership Practice: A Distributed Perspective." *Educational Researcher* 30, 3: 23–28.

Spillane, James, and Charles Thompson. 1997. "Reconstructing Conceptions of Local Capacity: The Local Education Agency's Capacity for Ambitious Instructional Reform." *Education Evaluation and Policy Analysis* 19, 2: 185–203.

Springboard Schools. 2006. *Minding the Gap: New Roles for School Districts in the Age of Accountability.* San Francisco: Springboard Schools.

Stecher, Brian, and George Bohrnstedt. 2002. *Class Size Reduction in California: Findings from 1999–00 and 2001–02.* Palo Alto, CA: Ed Source.

Steele, Claude M. 1997. "A Threat in the Air: How Stereotypes Shape the Intellectual Identities and Performance of Women and African-Americans." *American Psychologist* 52: 613–629.

Stone, Clarence, Jeffrey R. Henig, Bryan D. Jones, and Carol Pierannunzi. 2001. *Building Civic Capacity: The Politics of Reforming Urban Schools.* Lawrence: University Press of Kansas.

Tharp, Roland, and Ronald Gallimore. 1988. *Rousing Minds to Life: Teaching, Learning, and Schooling in Social Context.* New York: Cambridge University Press.

Thomas, Toch. 2008. *Rush to Judgment: Teacher Evaluation in Public Education.* Washington, DC: Public Sector.

Townsend, Barbara. 2000. "The Disproportionate Discipline of African-American Learners: Reducing School Suspensions and Expulsions," *Exceptional Children* 66: 381–391.

Tyack, David. 1974. *The One Best System: A History of American Urban Education.* Cambridge, MA: Harvard University Press.

Tyack, David, and Larry Cuban. 1995. *Tinkering Toward Utopia: A Century of Public School Reform.* Cambridge, MA: Harvard Education Press.

Valenzuela, Angela. 1999. *Subtractive Schooling.* Albany: State University of New York Press.

Vella, Jane. 2008. *On Teaching and Learning: Putting the Principles and Practices of Dialogue Education into Action.* San Francisco: Jossey-Bass.

Vinovskis, Maris. 1999. "Do Federal Compensatory Education Programs Really Work? A Brief Historical Analysis of Title I and Head Start." *American Journal of Education* 107: 187–209.

Weinstein, Rona. 2002. *Reaching Higher: The Power of Expectations in Schooling.* Cambridge, MA: Harvard University Press.

Wolfgang, Charles H. 2004. *Solving Discipline and Classroom Management Problems: Methods and Models for Today's Teachers,* sixth edition. Hoboken, NJ: John Wiley & Sons.

Yinger, John, ed. 2004. *Helping Children Left Behind: State Aid and the Pursuit of Educational Equity.* Cambridge, MA: MIT Press.

Young, Iris Marion. 2000. "Displacing the Distributive Paradigm." In David Johnson, ed., *Equality.* Indianapolis: Hackett Publishing.

Zeichner, Kenneth M. 1996. "Educating Teachers for Cultural Diversity," in Kenneth M. Zeichner, Mary Louise Gomez, and Susan Melnick, eds., *Preparing Teachers for Cultural Diversity.* New York: Teachers College Press.

Zuckerbrod, Nancy. 2008. "Six States to Design Own Plans for Fixing Schools." *Washington Post,* July 1.

INDEX

ABOUT THE AUTHORS

W. Norton Grubb is the David Pierpont Gardner Professor in Higher Education at the University of California, Berkeley. He is also the faculty coordinator of the Principal Leadership Institute, a program to prepare principals for urban schools. In addition to conducting wide-ranging research, he provides workshops for secondary and community college instructors and administrators, presenting different approaches to reform. He has also participated in public policy efforts such as the California Master Plan Commission and National Research Council Committee on high school motivation. His recent books include *The Education Gospel: The Economic Power of Schooling; Honored But Invisible: An Inside Look at Teaching in Community Colleges;* and *Learning to Work: The Case for Reintegrating Education and Job Training.*

Lynda Tredway is the coordinator of the Principal Leadership Institute. Before going to Berkeley she spent almost thirty years working with urban schools in Washington, D.C. She was formerly on the faculty of George Washington University, where she was project director for the Urban Initiative, a school-university partnership for preparing preservice teachers for urban schools. She has also served as a program director and lead teacher in the Washington, D.C., public schools. Her publications include *A Primer for Social Justice Educators and Community Mapping: A Curricular Guide for Teacher Educators*, from the Contextual Teaching and Learning Project of USDOE (with M. Freund).